Rhode Island

Rhode Island

Sylvia McNair

Children's Press®
A Division of Grolier Publishing
New York   London   Hong Kong   Sydney
Danbury, Connecticut

Frontispiece: Sachuest Point, Middletown

Front cover: Slater Mill National Historic Site

Back cover: Canoeing at Providence River Park

Consultant: Meredith Paine Sorozan, The Rhode Island Historical Society

Please note: All statistics are as up-to-date as possible at the time of publication.

Visit Children's Press on the Internet at http://publishing.grolier.com

Book production by Editorial Directions, Inc.

Library of Congress Cataloging-in-Publication Data

McNair, Sylvia.
    Rhode Island / Sylvia McNair.
        144 p. 24 cm. — (America the beautiful. Second series)
    Includes bibliographical references and index.
    Summary : Describes the geography, plants, animals, history, economy, language,
        religions, culture, sports, arts, and people of the state of Rhode Island.
    ISBN 0-516-21043-2
    1. Rhode Island Juvenile literature. [1. Rhode Island.] I. Title. II. Series.
F79.3.M38 2000
974.5—dc21   99-35216
                                                                                      CIP

Acknowledgments

I am grateful for the assistance of various people in the Rhode Island state government who supplied me with useful information. Special thanks go to Ann Wilkinson, who has traveled with me in much of New England and helped me in my research, and to Anna Idol for many years of assistance on a variety of projects.

Narragansett Bay

Rhode Island coastline

Mount Hope Bridge

Red chicken

Contents

Providence skyline

The Breakers

Young Rhode Islanders

Topiary at
Green Animals

CHAPTER ONE

The Ocean State

Rhode Island's official nickname is the Ocean State, because so much of its land lies along the Atlantic Ocean and its bays. If one could squeeze a piece of modeling clay shaped like Rhode Island into a perfect square, the boundary would be only about 140 miles (225 kilometers) long. But the shoreline of Rhode Island is more than twice that length. It meanders in and out of many inlets and bays and about thirty-six islands for a total of 384 miles (618 km).

In a sense, everything about Rhode Island is based on water. Roger Williams, founder of the state, selected a spot beside a spring of fresh, cool water and called his settlement Providence. Port cities that grew up beside deepwater harbors off Rhode Island's shores rapidly became world trading centers. Shipping, in turn, created a shipbuilding industry. The waters have also supplied an abundance of fish and seafood, sufficient for residents' own needs with plenty left over to sell.

Rhode Island's coastline is rugged and beautiful.

Opposite: Solitude at Sakonnet Point

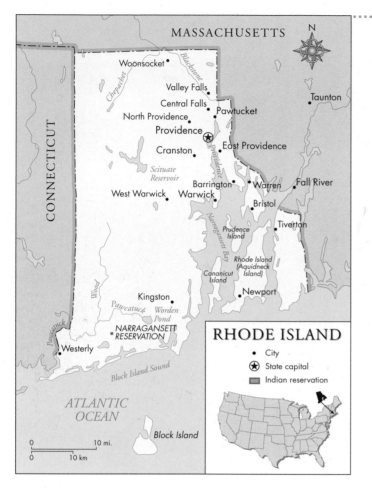

Geopolitical map of Rhode Island

Waterpower from the Blackstone River gave birth to Rhode Island's manufacturing industry. For many years, this state was the most industrialized in the nation. Industry, in turn, caused waves of immigration. The people from many lands who sailed across the ocean have given Rhode Island a rich and fascinating diversity.

And for more than 300 years, the waters of the Atlantic Ocean and its countless bays and inlets have given the people of Rhode Island incomparable places to play. Some of the richest people in America have chosen Rhode Island as a place to build luxurious vacation homes. Its residents, wherever they live, are never more than a few minutes away from a river, a bay, or an ocean beach.

A more popular nickname than Ocean State is Little Rhody, because this is the smallest of all fifty states. It covers only 1,231 square miles (3,188 square kilometer). Delaware, the next smallest, has twice as much land, and Alaska, the largest state, has almost 500 times as much. But small as Little Rhody is, its people have had a great deal to do with making the United States what it is today.

All Americans are proud of the nation's heritage of independence, but Rhode Islanders claim that theirs is the most indepen-

dent state of all. On May 4, 1776, Rhode Island declared its independence from Britain, two months before this colony was joined
by twelve others in agreeing to the Declaration of Independence.
The colony was founded on the principle of freedom of thought and
of religion—for all people.

A tall, gold-leafed bronze statue of a man overlooks the city of
Providence, Rhode Island. It tops the dome of the state capitol, a
beautiful marble building on the crest of Capitol Hill, and is known
as *Independent Man.*

Let's visit Little Rhody, the Ocean State, the "most independent" of the fifty states, and see how it came to be what it is today.

Independent Man **atop
the state capitol**

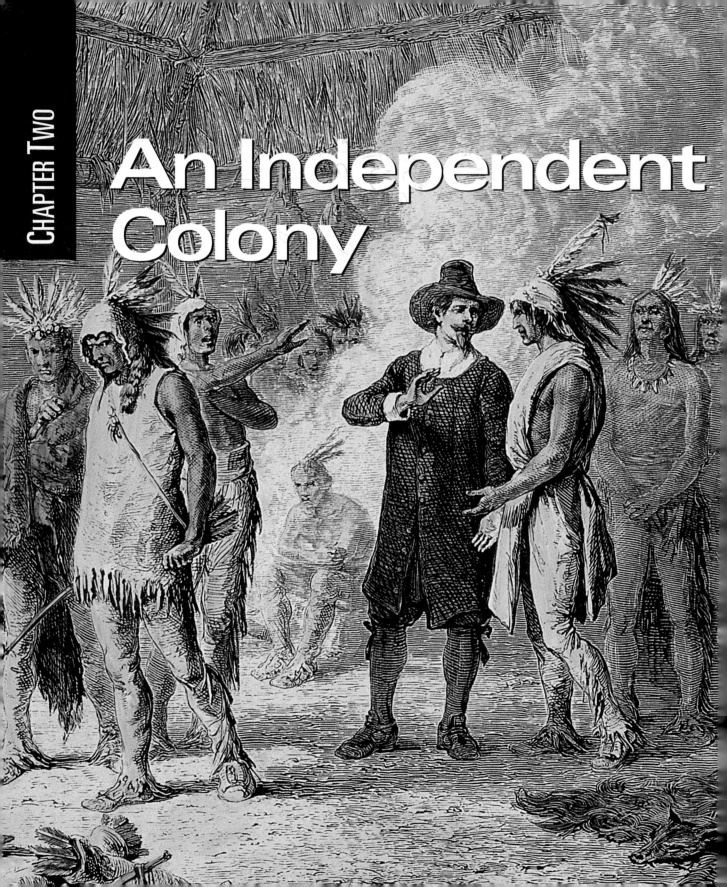

CHAPTER TWO

An Independent Colony

Imagine what New England was like before the Europeans arrived. There were no cities, hills and valleys were covered with thick forests, rivers and streams carried pure water to the ocean. The forests were full of wildlife and the waters teemed with fish.

According to archaeologists, Native Americans came into the New England region from the south and west about 12,000 years ago. They were few in number, and they had plenty of space for hunting, fishing, and gathering plants for food. These early inhabitants lived in small communities and hunting camps, made tools of stone, and built large fish traps, called weirs. Eventually, they began to cultivate crops—maize (corn), beans, squash, pumpkins, cucumbers, and tobacco.

The first encounters between Europeans and the Native Americans of New England occurred around A.D. 1500, soon after the voyages of Christopher Columbus to the Western Hemisphere. Explorers from England, France, and Portugal were excited about the prospect of land and riches to be found across the ocean. In 1524, Italian explorer Giovanni da Verrazzano sailed into what is now Narragansett Bay.

Unfortunately, the first meetings with Europeans were disastrous for the Native Americans. They had enjoyed fairly good

A group of Native Americans view the approach of a European ship.

Opposite: Roger Williams communicating with Native Americans

health before the newcomers arrived. Many diseases common in Europe, such as smallpox and measles, were unknown in the Americas. Some Europeans who had developed immunity to such diseases were carriers, and they exposed the Native Americans to these epidemic diseases for the first time. Thus, even before settlers arrived in New England, the native population had begun to shrink as a result of their contact with traders and fishing crews.

Roger Williams

In 1631, a young Englishman named Roger Williams came to Boston. He was twenty-eight years old. He was offered a job as an assistant pastor, but the way the Boston Church was being run did not seem quite right to him. It was too much like the Anglican Church he had left behind in England. Williams went down the coast to Plymouth, where he found a congregation that seemed more independent in thinking. However, the Boston people had influence in Plymouth, too, and he felt pressured to go along with ideas he didn't agree with. He left Plymouth and went to Salem.

Along with his ministerial work in Plymouth, Williams began trading and associating with Native Americans on Cape Cod—the Wampanoag. As he got to know them, he began to question the right of European colonists to come to this continent and help themselves to the land.

Roger Williams founded Rhode Island and supported religious tolerance.

All of the other colonists, without exception as far as we know, believed the English king had the "right of discovery" to land on this side of the ocean. It simply did not occur to them that the American Indians had claims to their own homelands. But Williams was troubled. He had studied the laws of contracts and land titles and he knew that the colonists had neither paid for any acreage nor obtained it by treaty.

At the same time, Williams was questioning some of the accepted religious doctrines of the time. One of his beliefs was especially alarming to the Pilgrims and Puritans. He thought there should be complete separation of church and state—that neither institution should meddle in the affairs of the other. Therefore, he argued, everyone should be free to worship—or even not to worship—as he or she pleased.

Most of the colonists in Massachusetts had braved the difficult voyage across the sea to have the freedom to worship as they pleased. But in no way were they ready to extend that privilege to others who had different beliefs. They were convinced that they alone had the one true faith. Roger Williams, to them, was a heretic, a dangerous dissenter.

Roger Williams was tried for his heresy and banished from the new colonies along Massachusetts Bay. By this time, he was thirty-three years old. Actually, his opponents intended to have him

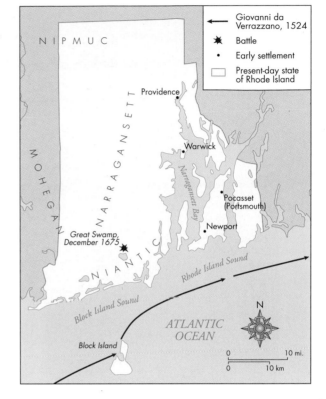

Exploration of Rhode Island

Roger Williams being welcomed by the Narragansett people

shipped back to England, but he heard about this plan. Wanting to stay in the colonies, he took off into the wilderness to the south in 1636. It was tough going, trudging through swamps and woods, paddling his canoe through chilly waters.

Williams believed that the Europeans and Native Americans were equals as human beings. The friendly Narragansett welcomed him to their lands. Some history books say that he purchased land from the Narragansett Indians. In his own writings, however, he said the land was a gift from the Indians, and that he gave back small gifts as a gesture of goodwill, not as payment for the land.

A "Lively Experiment"

Roger Williams and a few families from Salem found a spot near a good spring of freshwater and decided to settle there. He named their new home Providence and said he wished it to be a haven for people who wanted religious freedom. Soon there were three other settlements in the region that would later be known as Rhode Island. They were the sites of the present-day cities of Portsmouth, Newport, and Warwick.

Meanwhile, the colonies in Massachusetts and Connecticut joined together in an attempt to take over the Rhode Island settlements. To prevent this, Williams was able to obtain a charter from the English Parliament in 1644, for "the Providence Plan-

The area that Williams named Providence soon grew into a large and productive city.

Rhode Island, the Name

Where did the name *Rhode Island* come from? No one is absolutely sure. Some historians have given credit to the Italian explorer Giovanni da Verrazzano, who first spotted the large piece of land now known as Block Island (the southernmost island in the state) in 1524. He said it was similar in size to the Mediterranean island of Rhodes.

Others believe the name came from Adriaen Block, a Dutch explorer who described the piece of land in Narragansett Bay now commonly called Aquidneck Island as *Roodt Eylandt* (red island) for the color of its clay. Rhode Island became the official name of the colony in the charter of 1663. ■

King Charles II of England

tations in Narragansett Bay." Three years later, the four settlements united under this charter.

In 1663, the colony petitioned King Charles II for the right to continue the "lively experiment" of guaranteeing religious freedom to all settlers. The charter granted to the colony by the king was the basis of government in Rhode Island until 1843.

Rhode Island quickly became known as a haven for people persecuted elsewhere for their religious beliefs. Several groups with widely different ideas of worship settled in this young colony. They had spirited discussions and arguments about theology—each person freely expressing his or her own point of view. Years later, Roger Williams remembered these early years as "wonderful, searching, disputing, and dissenting times."

One group, the Antinomians, left Boston and parted company with the Puritans because they believed that obedience to God and conscience was more important than obeying laws made by human leaders. They settled in Pocasset, which was later named Portsmouth. Among them were Anne and William Hutchinson and their friend Mary Dyer. Others went to Newport. Samuel Gorton settled at first in Providence and later founded Warwick. He did not belong to any church, but conducted services in his own home.

In 1657, a group of Quaker missionaries arrived by ship in Newport. They made converts among some of the original settlers, and Newport soon became a center of Quakerism. Seventh-Day Baptists formed another group in Newport. Huguenots (French Protestants), persecuted for their beliefs in Catholic France, emigrated to Rhode Island. Forty-five of these families settled in what is now East Greenwich. Several Sephardic Jews arrived during the same period and they started a congregation in 1658.

Samuel Gorton founded the city of Warwick.

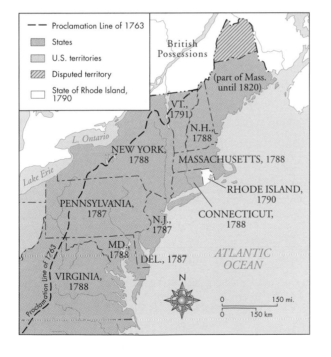

Historical map of Rhode Island

Mary Dyer

Mary Dyer, expelled from Boston by the Puritans for her religious beliefs, moved to Rhode Island with the Hutchinsons and their friends. She lived there for a few years and then returned to her native England. While there, she became acquainted with some Quakers and joined their group, called the Society of Friends. After seven years, she returned to America.

Once again Dyer aroused the wrath of the Puritans for publicly testifying to her faith. She returned to Boston often and was arrested each time. Finally, she was publicly hanged on Boston Common. ■

Roger Williams founded the first Baptist congregation in America. Williams, however, still questioning, left the church after only a few months. He never joined another church and called himself a "Seeker," a searcher for the truth. He used his influence in Rhode Island to promote tolerance toward people of all religions and races.

Historic Houses of Worship

Two houses of worship symbolize the principle of religious liberty that was protected from the very beginning of the Rhode Island colonies. Both the First Baptist Church (top left) in Providence and Touro Synagogue (top right) in Newport are more than 200 years old, and both are still used for services today.

The first Baptist Church in America, founded by Roger Williams and his companions in 1639, was erected in 1775. The auditorium is a square room with white walls, clear windows, and no crosses, statues, or icons. Fluted columns, each one a solid oak tree, are hand-carved to look like classical pillars. The church is one of the largest constructed in colonial America. Built to seat 1,200 people, it is used for Brown University's graduation exercises, as well as for regular church services.

The most striking ornamentation in the auditorium is a huge, gleaming, crystal chandelier. Given to the church in 1792, it was lit by candles until 1884, and then by gaslight until 1914, when it was converted to electricity.

Touro Synagogue in Newport is the oldest Jewish synagogue in the United States. Completed in 1763, it was the center of Jewish life in Newport. During the Revolutionary War many Jews moved away, and the synagogue was closed part of the time.

Many Newport buildings were damaged during the Revolutionary War. For several years, town meetings and sessions of the Rhode Island General Assembly were held in the synagogue.

President George Washington wrote a letter to the congregation in 1790. He included a statement about tolerance that is still the ideal for Americans: ". . . the Government of the United States . . . gives to bigotry no sanction, to persecution no assistance."

The exterior of Touro Synagogue is plain brick. Large windows and tall columns give the interior a spacious and airy look. In the Orthodox tradition, women sat in the gallery. On the main floor, men sat on a bench along the inside walls. ■

In the early years, some of the settlers were opposed to the idea of slavery. A law passed in the 1650s outlawed the keeping of any person in slavery for longer than ten years. This may have been the first antislavery law in the British colonies. But when the American colonies united shortly afterward, the law was nullified. Before long, Newport was the largest slaveholding town in New England and a major slave-trading port.

King Philip, chief of the Wampanoag

King Philip's War

Another early law prohibited the enslavement of Indians, but good relations between the settlers and Native Americans soon broke down. Roger Williams and several other prominent Rhode Islanders tried hard to promote friendly and peaceful relations with the Native Americans of southern New England. But more and more English settlers kept arriving and taking over lands owned by the Indians. Members of several tribes began to see a need to work together to resist the English expansion. In 1675, a young chief of the Wampanoag (Eastlanders) tribe organized a coalition with the Narragansett, Nipmuck, Mohegan, and Podunk. His name was Metacomet, and the settlers nicknamed him King Philip.

It is not clear which side fired the first shot, but after the death of one of the Native

Americans, the Indians launched attacks on fifty-two of the ninety towns in Massachusetts and Rhode Island. Twelve of the towns were wiped out, and at least two towns were burned to the ground. Male settlers were killed; women and children were taken prisoner.

The settlers raised an army and retaliated severely. In a battle called the Great Swamp Fight, they attacked an encampment near Kingston, Rhode Island. After nearly two years of fighting, most of the Nipmuck, Mohegan, and Podunk people were wiped out. Metacomet was brutally killed, and some 500 members of his tribe were sold into slavery in the West Indies. The conflict, remembered as King Philip's War, marked the end of cooperation between the settlers and the Native Americans.

Rhode Island Turns to Trade

Rhode Island and Connecticut were the only colonies that were never ruled by a governor appointed by the English king. They ran their own affairs from the start. In 1647, the four Rhode Island towns of Providence, Portsmouth, Newport, and Warwick met to set up a system of laws to govern the colony and to protect individual rights. Many of the principles established in this colony are the basis of the U.S. federal government today.

For many decades after King Philip's War, European countries fought one another over the lands in North America. Britain expected support from the colonies in the form of troops, provisions, and taxes. Rhode Island was reluctant to cooperate with England in these battles, however. Their fiercely independent spirit made Rhode Islanders feel they were self-sufficient and didn't need to be involved with the outside world. But as the population

Newport grew eventually into a beach resort.

increased, it became obvious that the colony's future depended on commerce and trade with other countries.

During the eighteenth century, Rhode Island developed into a major center of international trade and shipping. The towns, no longer simply a scattering of self-contained frontier settlements, began to work together to build an orderly and productive society. Roads, bridges, and ferries were built to help farmers transport their products to the seaports. Providence and Newport, as well as a half-dozen other towns around Narragansett Bay, became important market centers. Corn, beans, livestock, dairy products, and timber were major exports, along with bounty from the ocean—fish and whale products. These were exchanged for products from other North American colonies or for manufactured goods imported from England.

The harbor of Newport in 1730

But before long, Rhode Island merchants discovered a much more lucrative source of income—the so-called Triangle Trade. Ships began to sail a route that began in the West Indies, headed north to Newport and other New England ports, crossed the ocean to Africa, then returned to the West Indies. Molasses, made from sugar cane grown in the islands, was brought to Newport and used to make rum. The rum was taken to Africa where it was traded for black slaves. The slaves were brought to West Indies under unbelievably horrible conditions and sold for more molasses. By 1765, Rhode Island had twenty-one towns and a population of about

50,000. Its merchants owned a fleet of 500 ships, and about one-fourth of the colony's workers were seamen.

This was a colony founded on the ideal of human independence and freedom, but it was now getting rich by denying freedom to thousands of other humans.

The Road to Revolution

British officials were looking for ways to make more money out of their North American colonies. They wanted to keep them dependent on the mother country. One way to do this was to force the colonies to import all their manufactured goods from England. A series of laws were passed forbidding the manufacture in the colonies of woolen goods, of hats, and eventually of iron products.

Britain then passed the Molasses Act to force the colonists to buy molasses only from the British West Indies. But these British colonies did not produce enough molasses to satisfy New England's demand—and the prices were high. So ship captains turned to smuggling.

In 1764, British naval vessels entered Narragansett Bay in search of smugglers. As one of the British ships started to leave Newport harbor, Rhode Island troops fired a cannon shot that hit its mainsail. Some claimed later that this was the first shot of the Revolutionary War.

Soon Parliament passed another tax law. The Stamp Act of 1765 imposed a tax on almost every paper item imported to the colonies, including legal documents and playing cards. All the colonies were outraged—none more than Rhode Island. Newporters reacted with several acts of open defiance against British authority. They burned a boat from a British ship in 1765 and set fire to a patrol ship in 1769. Three years later, John Brown, a Providence merchant, led an attack party to burn the British ship *Gaspee.*

When the British imposed a tax on tea, the colonists' favorite beverage, Bostonians held their famous Tea Party and dumped a shipload of it into the harbor. Britain retaliated by closing the port of Boston. The Rhode Island General Assembly decided it was time to join with the other colonies and take some drastic steps. In 1774, a Continental Congress convened in Philadelphia "to con-

The burning of the British ship *Gaspee* in 1772

Abraham Whipple, the commander of the first ships in what became the U.S. Navy

sider the proper means for the preservation of the rights and liberties of the colonies." Rhode Island representatives were there.

The Continental Congress met twice in Philadelphia. Delegates were beginning to see that war with Britain was inevitable. They organized an army and appointed George Washington as commander in chief. Fighting began in Concord, Massachusetts, and nearby Lexington on April 19, 1775.

Rhode Island's general assembly voted to raise an army to defend the colony. The assembly also outfitted two ships, under the command of Captain (later promoted to Commodore) Abraham Whipple. This was, in effect, the first American navy.

A few Tories, people who were still loyal to Britain, left the colony. Quakers, true to their pacifist beliefs, refused to take part in fighting, but most of them sympathized with the colonists' cause. On May 4, 1776, two months before the Continental Congress proclaimed the Declaration of Independence in Philadelphia, the Rhode Island general assembly officially voted to discontinue the colony's allegiance to the king. Since 1884, this date has been celebrated as Rhode Island Independence Day. Two months later, the assembly changed the word "colony" in their charter to "state."

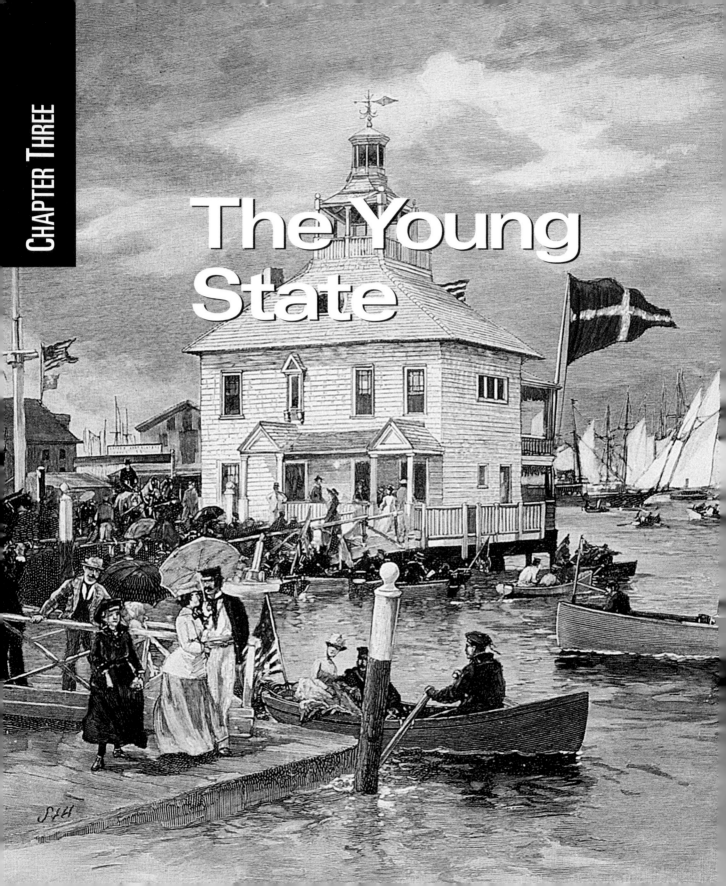

CHAPTER THREE

The Young State

n May 1775, General Nathanael Greene of Warwick led 1,000 Rhode Island troops to join the Continental Army in Boston. Fighting continued for the next six years. For three of those years, British forces occupied the city of Newport and nearly destroyed it. From Newport, the troops tramped over the Rhode Island countryside, helping themselves to crops and livestock and turning farmlands into fortifications. Refugees crowded into Providence.

Rhode Island troops took part in every major battle of the Revolution, though only one battle was fought on Rhode Island soil, in 1778. With the aid of French allies, American troops tried to recapture Newport. They were not successful, but the British voluntarily left the state a year later. The war finally ended with a British surrender, and a peace treaty was signed in 1783.

Nathanael Greene

Opposite: A Newport yachting club in the 1880s

Post-War Problems

Affairs in Rhode Island were in a shambles. The state had gone deeply into debt to finance its part in the fighting. The prosperous shipping trade was nearly dead. The beautiful city of Newport was almost in ruins.

The spirit of cooperation that had led Rhode Islanders into battle with the other colonists did not survive the war. Once again, the spirit of independence was of first importance. When delegates of the other twelve states met in Philadelphia's Independence Hall in 1778 to set up a new federal government, no representative was there from Rhode Island. The state was very reluctant to surrender any power to a central government.

A 1778 battle off the coast of Rhode Island

George Washington and other federal leaders were shocked at Rhode Island's attitude. They tried to pressure the state into ratifying the new Constitution, but Rhode Islanders had several objections. They disagreed with the other states on taxation policies, and they did not want representation in Congress to be based on population, because their state had the fewest people. In addition, they wanted the Constitution to include guarantees of religious liberty and other civil rights, and some wanted slavery to be abolished.

By 1790, all twelve of the other original states had ratified the new Constitution, but Rhode Island still held out. Finally, a compromise was reached on the issue of representation. Rhode Island would have two senators, the same as every other state, but membership in the House of Representatives would be on the basis of population. Rhode Island would have only one representative. And the new Constitution would be amended immediately to include a Bill of Rights.

On December 15, 1791, ten amendments to the U.S. Constitution, known as the Bill of Rights, became law. Roger Williams

Rhode Island Joins the Union

The people of Rhode Island were divided over the issue of joining the new Union. The majority, called the Country Party, wanted to go it alone, independent of the other colonies. People in the large towns, for the most part, disagreed. At one point, leaders from both Providence and Newport threatened to secede from the state and join the Union on their own.

Compromises eventually persuaded enough people to bring about a victory for statehood. On May 29, 1790, Rhode Island became the last of the thirteen original colonies to join the Union, and even then it was a close vote—34 to 32. ■

Oliver Hazard Perry

A fourteen-year-old boy from South Kingstown, Rhode Island, joined the U.S. Navy in 1799. He served as a midshipman under his father, who was a naval officer. He served on ships in the Caribbean and Mediterranean Seas. Later, Lieutenant Oliver Hazard Perry became famous during a conflict with Britain known as the War of 1812.

Perry commanded a fleet of nine small ships in Lake Erie, off the coast of Ohio. His ships blockaded a British fleet at the western end of the lake. When the *Lawrence,* Perry's flagship, was disabled, the lieutenant transferred to a small boat and rowed to another ship. The British surrendered after a very short battle. Perry's message to his military commander, General (later President) William Henry Harrison, included these famous words: "We have met the enemy, and they are ours."

Today, Put-in-Bay is a popular vacationing spot for people who arrive in private boats or ferries from the Ohio mainland. A major attraction is Perry's Victory and International Peace Memorial, a 352-foot (107-m) granite column. From the top, visitors have a panoramic view of Lake Erie and its Canadian and U.S. shores.

Perry died in 1819 and is buried in Newport, Rhode Island. ∎

had devoted his whole life to the promotion of religious freedom and the separation of church and state. Now, 155 years after he started his settlement, these rights were guaranteed for the new nation.

Some Still Not Free

The Triangle Trade (which included slave-trading) had helped to make Rhode Island merchants and shipowners rich in the years leading up to the American Revolution. But some Rhode Islanders—especially the Quakers—believed that slavery was evil.

The Dorr Rebellion

Thomas Wilson Dorr (right) was a member of the Rhode Island state legislature from 1834 to 1837. Educated at Harvard, he was an attorney and an enthusiastic reformer. He worked to improve public education, to promote the antislavery movement, and to reform the voting laws.

At this time, Rhode Island was still governed under the charter granted by England in 1663. Many people, Dorr among them, saw a need for a new constitution that would give people more say in their government.

Dorr and his followers called a People's Convention, where they drew up a People's Constitution. Another group wrote a so-called Landowners' Constitution. The state supreme court declared that the People's Constitution was not valid, but the Dorrites ignored the ruling. They held a statewide election and inaugurated Thomas Dorr governor of the state.

Dorr was convicted of treason and sentenced to life imprisonment but he was released after serving one year. His ideas for voting reforms were partially written into a new state constitution, ratified in 1843.

The new constitution said that ownership of property was no longer required of adult male voters. If they were born in the United States, they could qualify by having served in the militia or by paying a $1 fee for registration. Black citizens, as well as white, could vote, but foreign-born naturalized citizens were still required to own property to vote. ◾

Antislavery reformers succeeded in passing a law forbidding Rhode Island vessels to engage in the slave trade, but that law was difficult to enforce. The trade was very profitable, and wealthy merchants found ways to get around the law. However, the ownership of slaves was gradually abolished in Rhode Island.

African-Americans and Native Americans were welcomed into churches, but they were not accepted as social or political equals. As in other young states, only white male property owners had the right to vote before 1843.

Samuel Slater was instrumental in the U.S. Industrial Revolution.

The Industrial Revolution

Before the American Revolution, Rhode Island had been more concerned with expanding its world trade than with politics. When the war was over, however, Rhode Islanders again became preoccupied with economic matters. Shipping and trade were still important, but the business world was changing. Rhode Island was at the forefront of the change.

One man has been called the Father of America's Industrial Revolution. His name was Samuel Slater, and he started his revolution in Rhode Island.

Slater, a young Englishman, had worked in cotton-spinning mills for several years. He understood machinery, and he believed he could make a fortune in America. There were no cloth-making factories in the states, and it was against the law to export machinery from England. The English manufacturers wanted to keep their secrets to themselves.

The first cotton mill in the United States, founded by Slater along the Blackstone River

The Browns of Rhode Island

The New England colonies of Massachusetts, Connecticut, and Rhode Island produced some of the remarkable families that shaped the early history of the United States. Important names repeated through many generations include Adams in Massachusetts, Wolcott in Connecticut, and Brown in Rhode Island.

In one generation, four Brown brothers made their mark. They were enthusiastic supporters of the American Revolution. Nicholas Brown (above), a mer-chant, headed their company. His brother John sent merchant ships to Africa, Europe, Asia, and the Caribbean islands. Joseph Brown was an architect who designed some of the buildings in Providence. Moses Brown (below) was an industrialist who helped William Slater start the first cotton mills.

Moses Brown was also an abolitionist and he opposed his brother John's involvement in the slave trade. He was co-founder of the Providence

Society for Abolishing the Slave Trade. This society not only worked to persuade Congress to take action but also gave legal aid to slaves and established schools for blacks. His son was also interested in education and supported a school called the Friends School, now known as Moses Brown School.

Nicholas Brown gave major support to Rhode Island College, as did later generations of the family. The college was later renamed Brown University.

Two Brown homes are still standing in Providence. One was John Brown's elegant colonial home, which now belongs to the Rhode Island Historical Society and is open to the public. Another, the Nightingale-Brown House, was owned by the Brown family for almost 200 years and now belongs to Brown University. ■

Slater, however, was sure he could duplicate the machinery he had used—and even improve on it. He left England and soon teamed up with Moses Brown, a wealthy Rhode Island merchant. Before long, Slater had a factory running. In 1790, the business was producing the first cotton thread in America made by water-

A group of young girls who worked in a Rhode Island textile mill

powered machinery. Within only twenty-five years, there were 165 cotton mills in New England.

Rhode Island had the three elements needed for the growth of factories: capital, power, and labor. Men who had made fortunes in trade supplied the capital. Water from rivers and streams could be harnessed to manufacture power. And cheap labor was plentiful. Unfortunately, many of the cheap laborers were children. It would be many years before laws were passed to protect children from being forced to work long hours in factories.

The manufacture of cotton thread was only the beginning of Rhode Island's industry. Textiles woven from the thread soon followed. Waterpower gave way to steam power. Machinery, engines, and tools, as well as factories to build them, were needed, as were new facilities for banking and insurance. Before long, Providence was home to factories turning out jewelry and flatware, and it is still a leading center for these products.

By the onset of the Civil War, Rhode Island was the most industrialized state in the Union. More than 50 percent of the workers in Rhode Island were employed in manufacturing, while only 10 percent were in farming and only 3 percent in the maritime trade. Providence was the center for shipping the state's manufactured goods to markets, both by sea and rail. Newport was no longer Rhode Island's largest and most influential city.

Two young boys who made money by selling newspapers and shining shoes

Immigration

The demand for manufactured goods, especially textiles, grew rapidly during the nineteenth century. Factories expanded, more factories were built, and an increasing number of workers were needed to run the machinery. There simply weren't enough people available in Rhode Island.

The news was heard in Europe—whole families could get work in America! The first wave of immigration came from Ireland in the 1820s, and the Irish kept coming for the rest of the century. After a few years, French Canadians got the word too. Still later, good-sized groups of Italians and Portuguese arrived. Fathers, mothers, and children all worked in the mills. By 1900, descendants of the original Yankee settlers were in the minority in Rhode Island.

Rhode Island was founded as a haven for all religions, but during its first 250 years, most of the people were Protestants. By 1900, Roman Catholics were in the majority.

The Civil War

Rhode Island had strong economic ties with the Southern states and did not want to go to war with them. The state government sent five delegates to a peace convention in Virginia to try to avert a war over slavery. At the same time, the citizens of the state did not want to see the United States torn apart, and when war broke out, a large number of volunteers joined the Union army.

Rhode Island prospered greatly from the war. Soon more of its people were rich, or at least comfortably well off, than ever before.

The Gilded Age in Newport

Rhode Islanders like to brag that their state was the nation's first resort. They report that the Italian explorer Giovanni da Verrazzano took a "two-week vacation" sailing around the islands in Narragansett Bay in the 1500s. That may be stretching it a bit, but Rhode Island was, in fact, a popular destination for wealthy vacationers very early in its history.

Even before the American Revolution, plantation owners from Charleston, South Carolina, and Savannah, Georgia, began coming to Newport to escape the steamy southern summers. During the 1840s, its seaside also became a popular getaway spot for Bostonian writers and other intellectuals.

Newport oceanfront homes in 1858

The Breakers

The Breakers, Newport's largest and most expensive mansion, is now Rhode Island's most popular tourist attraction. From floor to ceiling, the opulence and glamour are overwhelming.

Cornelius Vanderbilt II had the mansion built in the 1890s. His grandfather, Commodore Vanderbilt, had made a huge fortune in steamships, railroads, and the fur trade. The seventy-room summer cottage was designed by an American architect, but its style is similar to sixteenth-century Italian palaces. Thirty-three of the rooms housed the huge staff of servants who traveled to Newport with the Vanderbilts for the social season. Now owned by the Preservation Society of Newport County, The Breakers has been open to visitors on guided tours since 1948.

It is hard to know where to look when touring the house, since nearly every inch of every surface is intricately carved, painted, or gilded. The main rooms gleam with polished alabaster and marble, gold and bronze accents, red velvet draperies and upholstery, and glittering crystal chandeliers. One can imagine the rooms filled with dancing couples—New York's most prominent and wealthy tycoons, the ladies in splendid silk designer gowns adorned with diamonds, rubies, and emeralds.

Outside, visible through large glass doors, are panoramic views of the ocean. Waves crashing against the shore in rough weather gave the mansion its name. ■

Later it became the chosen retreat of men who made tremendous fortunes during the boom period of the Industrial Revolution. Some called them New York tycoons. Critics called them "robber barons." For about seventy-five years, some of the wealthiest people in America spent part of their time in Newport. Many built second homes here. They called them "summer cottages." In size and decor, they were truly mansions. Filled with priceless paintings, sculpture, and antiques, the houses were surrounded by acres of formal gardens. The owners arrived by yacht or private railroad car, bringing dozens of family members, friends, and servants with them.

During the 1890s, often called the Gay Nineties, the Astors, the Vanderbilts, the Belmonts, and other members of so-called high society spent fortunes on having a good time in Newport. They hosted dinners, parties, and elaborate balls for hundreds of guests. Guest lists were selected from a social register that included only the so-called Four Hundred most important families. The amount they spent on a single party could have supported thousands of their factory workers for years.

CHAPTER FOUR

The Twentieth Century

Rhode Island attracted many wealthy people.

Rhode Island was rich and powerful as the twentieth century began. The factories were doing well; the manufacturers were as influential in politics as in business.

Unfortunately, much of the state's prosperity depended on the textile industry. And factory owners were beginning to discover that it was more profitable to manufacture wool and cotton cloth in the South than in New England. The climate was better, which meant lower overhead costs, and southern workers accepted lower wages than the northern factory employees.

Opposite: Mount Hope Bridge

Rhode Island's economy began a downward slide, which was temporarily reversed during World War I (1914–1918). Shortly after the war ended, however, the United States was hit by a severe recession. Some mills closed, and workers in other mills had to take sharp cuts in pay. Labor unions had never been strong in Rhode Island, but now the workers were desperate. With the leadership of two textile workers' unions, thousands of employees went out on strike.

After a long struggle, mill owners agreed not to cut wages further. But as wages and working conditions improved in New England, more of the employers simply transferred their operations to the south.

By the mid-twenties, Rhode Island was a divided state. On one side were the descendants of immigrant families—working class, underprivileged, and mostly Democrats. On the other were the more affluent and powerful people. They were the owners and managers of businesses, came from old Yankee stock, and voted Republican.

New Problems

The next few years brought one problem after another to the people of Rhode Island. First was the stock-market crash of 1929, which ushered in the long, hard years of the Great Depression. Labor problems continued to plague the textile industry, and factories continued to close or move away. Then, in 1938, nature struck Rhode Island a massive blow. A disastrous hurricane and tidal wave killed 258 people and caused millions of dollars worth of property damage.

During World War II (1939–1945), Rhode Island once again became an important part of the nation's arsenal, a source for manufacturing military equipment. Factories also produced chemicals, machinery, and electronics. Quonset Point Naval Station brought many wartime jobs to the state. A famous type of temporary shelter, known as the Quonset hut, was developed at the air station.

A textile mill in Woonsocket, 1940

The aftermath of the 1938 hurricane that hit the Rhode Island coast

After the war, however, many industries closed and the textile industry continued to shrink. By the late 1940s, the state's unemployment rate reached a high of 17 percent. From 1945 to 1973, the U.S. Navy was the largest single employer in the state of Rhode Island.

More hurricanes hit the state in the 1940s and 1950s, but none as destructive as the one in 1938. A huge hurricane barrier has now been built by the U.S. Army Corps of Engineers to protect downtown Providence from hurricane damage.

Politics

The Yankee-dominated Republican Party had held nearly complete control of Rhode Island politics for the last half of the nineteenth century. But this began to change as large numbers of American-born descendants of immigrants—especially the Irish—grew old enough to vote. At the turn of the century, there were two major, sharply divided, political groups—Protestant Republicans and Irish Catholic Democrats.

Theodore Francis Green

Visitors who come to Rhode Island by air usually land at Theodore Francis Green Airport. This gateway was named for a native son of Providence who represented his state in the U.S. Senate for twenty-four years.

Theodore Francis Green was born in Providence in 1867 of old-line Yankee stock. His ancestors had lived in the state since before the American Revolution. He was educated in the traditional Yankee way, earning degrees from Brown University and Harvard Law School. As a successful lawyer, businessman, and banker, Green became a millionaire.

Green's politics were not those of a traditional upper-class Yankee, however. He was elected to the state senate in 1906 on the Democratic ticket and remained active in that party for the rest of his life. Green's influence was a major factor in persuading the Irish Democrats to welcome other ethnic groups into the Irish-dominated party.

Elected as governor in 1932, Green served for four years. He initiated many progressive reforms for the state and helped his party gain control of the state legislature and judiciary.

Governor Green then ran for the U.S. Senate. He held that seat until 1961, when he decided not to run for re-election. He left the Senate at the age of ninety-three, the oldest person ever to have served in that office. His record stood until recently, when Senator Strom Thurmond of South Carolina surpassed it. ■

Democrats began to make political gains in the 1920s and 1930s, and the Great Depression contributed to this trend. Jobs were scarce and working conditions were harsh. As a result, labor unions grew stronger. The descendants of French-Canadian and Italian immigrants, who had traditionally voted Republican, began to side with the Irish.

When Democrat Franklin Delano Roosevelt was elected president in 1932, Rhode Island chose a Democratic governor as well—Theodore Francis Green. Democrats won most of the gubernatorial elections in the state for the next few decades. Lively competition between the two parties marked elections toward the end of the century.

A Changing Scene

The Industrial Revolution in the United States, which began in Rhode Island, brought great changes to people's everyday lives during the nineteenth century. The last half of the twentieth century was another period of transition. The state could no longer depend on textiles as its main source of income. Other manufactured products and service industries increased in importance.

The water surrounding Rhode Island is a laboratory for many kinds of scientific research. The University of Rhode Island has one of the finest programs for oceanographic research in the United States. The U.S. Public Health Service has a shellfish laboratory at Saunderstown. The U.S. Bureau of Sports Fisheries and Wildlife runs a biological laboratory at the same research center.

The revitalization of Providence has done much to stimulate the state economy.

Hope

"Hope" is the motto that appears on the Rhode Island state flag. In spite of economic and social problems facing the state, Rhode Islanders still have hope. In the 1960s, new roads and freeways helped make travel to and through the state easier. In 1969, a new bridge spanning Narragansett Bay opened and the section of Inter-state 95 crossing the state was completed. Among other benefits, these improvements in transportation helped bring more tourists to the state. In 1998, an estimated 14 million travelers visited Rhode Island.

Optimism in the city of Providence has led to a huge revital- ization program over the past twenty years. Thousands of historic buildings have been preserved and restored, including 5,000 now listed on the National Register of Historic Places. Old houses, public buildings, and business structures have been brought back to their original beauty. The massive changes include uncovering and cleaning up the rivers, beautifying the shores, rerouting streets and building new hotels, a convention center, and a large downtown shopping mall.

CHAPTER FIVE

The Land and Living Things

Rhode Island's rocky shore

Tens of thousands of years ago, a huge mass of ice began to move south from Canada. It completely covered the area that is now New England. The glacier, a huge slow-moving river of ice, cut grooves in the bedrock and carved out hills. It churned up sand, clay, and rocks and carried them along with it. Eventually, the ice began to melt and move back northward. Rivers formed from the melting ice. The water washed silt, sand, and gravel onto plains, threw up rocky cliffs, dug out ponds and lakes, and cut many channels to the sea. It also created a large bay with a jagged coastline—Rhode Island's Narragansett Bay.

Rhode Island is tucked away in the southern part of New England, bounded by Connecticut on the west, Massachusetts on the north and east, and the Atlantic Ocean on the south. The state is divided into two land regions. The Coastal Lowlands, which cover

Opposite: Sunset on Narragansett Bay

more than half of Rhode Island, are part of a region that stretches along the entire New England coast. The Eastern New England Upland extends from Connecticut and Rhode Island to Maine. This region, also called the Western Rocky Upland in Rhode Island, occupies the northwestern third of the state.

People who have never been to Rhode Island find it hard to believe how small it really is. The longest distance in the state, from north to south, is only 59 miles (95 km), and a mere 40 miles (64 km) from east to west. Drivers can easily cross the entire state in any direction in less than an hour—if there are no traffic jams. Many metropolitan areas (cities plus their suburbs) cover more territory than Rhode Island's 1,231 square miles (3,188 sq km). The state is also quite flat—Jerimoth Hill, its highest point, is only 812 feet (248 meters) above sea level.

Rhode Island's soil is fertile, but very rocky, which partly explains why agriculture gave way to industry early in the state's history. A variety of minerals is found in the state, but only sand and gravel are mined commercially. Coal, graphite, bog iron, quartzite, limestone, and granite were all mined in the past.

The Coastal Lowlands

More than half of Rhode Island's mainland is the Coastal Lowlands, including the narrow strip of land east of Narragansett Bay, the

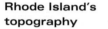

Rhode Island's topography

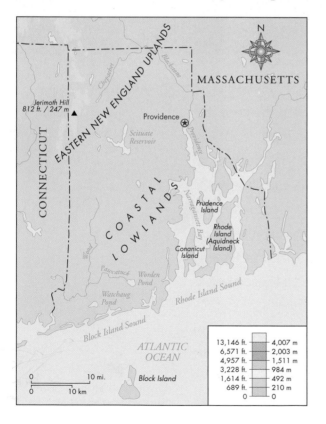

thirty-five islands in the bay, and Block Island. The lowlands are made up of sandy beaches, rocky cliffs, lagoons, saltwater ponds, and low plains. East of the bay are low slopes with very few trees. Hills are a slightly higher and forested on the western side.

Beaches do not stay put. Waves and currents move the sand and change the coastline. When the weather is calm and fair, sand is washed ashore and brought down from rivers, tending to make the beaches larger. Storms, on the other hand, usually sweep some of the sand into the ocean. This is called erosion. Often the sand swept from one stretch of beach is eventually deposited in another spot.

Block Island is part of the Coastal Lowlands.

Salt Ponds, Tide Pools, and Salt Marshes

Coastal lagoons, or salt ponds, are separated from the open ocean by barrier beaches. Freshwater is fed into them by rivers from the mainland, and saltwater flows in from the ocean through breaks in the beaches. These salty lagoons are very shallow, so the sunlight helps eelgrass to grow thickly. The salt ponds are important habitats for many fish and shellfish, as well as for waterfowl. More than 300 species of birds have been spotted in some of the lagoons along the coast.

When the tide goes out, it leaves pools behind in rocky stretches of shoreline. These natural aquariums are home to all kinds of interesting little creatures. Algae, mussels, and sea anemones cling to the rocks. Barnacles and periwinkles move about in search of food. Crabs, snails, small fish, and marine insects also find shelter in tide pools.

Salt marshes are wetlands near the ocean. Certain kinds of grass and hay thrive in the rich, boggy soil. Insects eat the grass, while tiny fish and shellfish find algae to feed on. Crabs feast on the smaller creatures, and they in turn provide food for shorebirds, mice, and other small mammals. ■

A string of barrier beaches lies off the south shore of Rhode Island. These are narrow, long ridges of sand and gravel, partially separated from the mainland by lagoons, wetlands, tidal inlets, and estuaries. An estuary is an arm of the sea.

Narragansett Bay is Rhode Island's most important natural feature. It is a 28-mile (45-km)-long estuary. On the Atlantic Coast of the United States, only Chesapeake Bay is a larger estuary than Narragansett. A large variety of plants and marine animals thrive in the bay, which is constantly fed freshwater from rivers and rainfall. Fishing, especially for shellfish, is an important industry in the bay.

Narragansett Bay is 28 miles (45 km) long.

Ports in Providence and Quonset Point/Davisville are important centers of maritime commerce. Transportation via Rhode Island's rivers and the Narragansett Bay was a large factor in the growth of industry in the state.

The bay is also an important recreational asset. Its 256 miles (412 km) of shoreline make it easily accessible by land from all of southern New England,

One of Providence's many marinas

and boaters from up and down the Atlantic coast visit it each year.

Rhode Island's Geographical Features

Total area; rank	1,231 sq. mi. (3,188 sq km); 50th
Land; rank	1,045 sq. mi. (2,707 sq km); 50th
Water; rank	186 sq. mi. (482 sq km); 48th
Inland water; rank	168 sq. mi. (435 sq km); 46th
Coastal water; rank	18 sq. mi. (47 sq km); 20th
Geographic center	Kent, 1 mile (1.6 km) southwest of Crompton
Highest point	Jerimoth Hill, 812 feet (248 m) above sea level
Lowest point	Sea level along the Atlantic coast
Largest city	Providence
Population; rank	1,005,984 (1990 census); 43rd
Record high temperature	104°F (40°C) at Providence on August 2, 1975
Record low temperature	−23°F (−31°C) at Kingston on January 11, 1942
Average July temperature	71°F (22°C)
Average January temperature	29°F (−2°C)
Average annual precipitation	44 inches (112 cm)

Bird Sanctuaries

Bird sanctuaries on Aquidneck and Conanicut Islands are established on land that was once cleared for farming. More than 100 acres (40 ha) on Conanicut are occupied by the Conanicut Island Sanctuary and the Audubon Society's Marsh Meadows Wildlife Preserve. Herons, egrets, and ibis are among the wading birds that build their nests on the islands. A large marsh on Conanicut is their major feeding ground. Several varieties of ducks also stop by for food during the winter.

Norman Bird Sanctuary in Middletown, once part of a large farm, is now one of the largest forested spots on Aquidneck Island. Three rock ridges, with valleys between, cut through the preserve. Scrubby vegetation grows on the ridges while rich forests, dotted with ponds and wetlands, fill the valleys. Nelson Pond is the site of an old slate quarry.

One field is especially popular with American woodcocks. In early spring, bird-watchers come to see these birds perform an unusual mating ritual. The male (right) catches the attention of female birds by sitting on the ground and making a buzzing sound. Then he swoops up nearly 30 feet (9 m) into the air and zigzags back down, twittering loudly.

Hanging Rock is a huge cliff overlooking the Atlantic Ocean. A popular Harvest Fair is held on the sanctuary grounds each autumn. ■

Eastern New England Upland

The Eastern New England Upland is a region of small valleys, rolling hills, lakes, reservoirs, and ponds. The elevation rises from about 200 feet (61 m) to a little more than 800 feet (244 m).

About 60 percent of Rhode Island's land is forested. When the Europeans arrived, they found dense woodlands, which they quickly set about clearing for farms. Much of the forest was gone by the end of the 1700s, but the Industrial Revolution proved to be a good thing for the forests. Agriculture was no longer as profitable for Rhode Islanders as the factories were. Fields and orchards were abandoned; grass, then shrubs, and finally trees took over the space.

Almost all of the forests that cover the state today are called "second-growth" forests—trees that have grown on former farm-land. More than half the trees are deciduous—trees that lose their leaves each year. Among them are oaks, maples, hickories, and birches. Evergreens, or conifers, include pines, spruces, cedars, and hemlocks.

A major enemy of Rhode Island trees is the gypsy moth. It was first identified in the state in 1901 and has reappeared several times since then. The gypsy moth is a pest that can strip a tree of all its leaves in a few weeks. Forestry authorities keep a constant watch for this enemy of the trees.

A forest of white pines

Rivers and Lakes

The Blackstone River has been a major factor in the state's industrial development. Dams in the river created millponds that furnished the energy to power the factories. Mills and mill villages sprang up along the river shores. Six cities grew up in the valley.

Flowing southeast from near Worcester, Massachusetts, the Blackstone enters Rhode Island just north of Woonsocket. As it continues on toward Narragansett Bay, past the industrial cities of Central Falls and Pawtucket, its name changes to the Pawtucket, then to the Seekonk. The

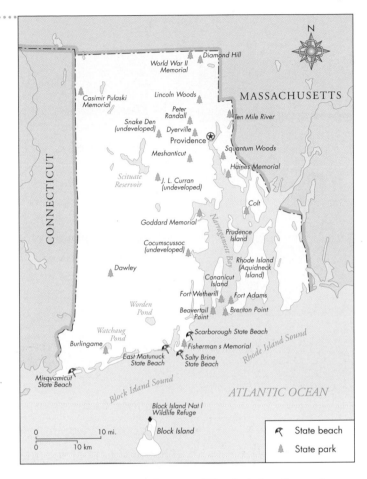

Rhode Island's parks and forests

The Blackstone River has been a major factor in Rhode Island's industrial growth.

The Sage of the Wilderness

The Reverend William Blackstone was the first resident of Boston. He was not happy with the Church of England, to which he belonged, but he was equally troubled by Puritan doctrine. He sold his farm and traveled, riding on a white bull. He built a cottage on a plateau overlooking a river in what is now Rhode Island. Roger Williams has gone down in history as the founder of Rhode Island, but Blackstone actually set-tled there before him. The two men became close friends.

Blackstone was a well-educated man who brought nearly 200 books with him to his new home. That was an exceedingly large library for the Americas. He became known in the region as the "Sage of the Wilderness." He lived in the valley, known today as the Blackstone River Valley, until his death, at the age of eighty. ■

part called the Seekonk River is saltwater—actually an arm of the bay.

Close to the state line, the Blackstone falls over a dam, past boulders and wooded slopes, then cuts through a rock-lined gorge. One of the most spectacular views in the state can be seen from an overlook. Blackstone Gorge is the only spot in Rhode Island where people can enjoy whitewater canoeing.

Other principal rivers are the Providence—also a saltwater river—and the Pawcatuck. The Pawcatuck flows through south-western Rhode Island to the Connecticut border.

There are 357 freshwater ponds, lakes, and reservoirs in this small state. Fish, frogs, and turtles make their homes in ponds. Ducks, swans, swallows, and kingfishers swim in the ponds along with beavers, muskrats, minks, and river otters.

Salamanders, wood frogs, and toads like to live for a short time

in vernal pools. These are temporary bodies of water that exist only in the spring. They are formed by rains and snowmelt.

A peaceful place along the Barrington River

Animal Life

Besides the abundance of marine life in Rhode Island's waters, quite a few land animals and birds can be found throughout rural areas. Common mammals are rabbits, squirrels, skunks, foxes, raccoons, opossums, and white-tailed deer. After the disappearance of the larger wild animals, such as wolves and mountain

lions, coyotes moved in. They are natural predators and pose some danger to small household pets.

More than 250 bird species can be spotted in the state. More than half of these are residents who build their nests here; the others are migrants who pass through in spring and fall. Large flocks of waterfowl live in Narragansett Bay and in coves and salt ponds.

Rabbits are among the animals that live in Rhode Island.

Block Island

Block Island was named for the Dutch explorer Adriaen Block, who stopped on the island in 1614. It lies only 9 miles (14 km) south of the mainland of Rhode Island, but it seems like a different world. It is sometimes described as being shaped like a pork chop with a big bite in the middle. That "bite" is a bay called the Great Salt Pond. It has a harbor where large sailing boats can tie up. Visitors come by ferry from Connecticut, Long Island, and mainland Rhode Island ports. Travelers hike on scenic trails or ride bikes along paths, climb rolling hills and stroll across moors, pausing to enjoy the beaches and picturesque bluffs and quiet coves. Residents claim there are 365 ponds on the island, one for each day of the year. ■

Climate

Rhode Island's climate is usually a little milder than in most of New England. Temperatures are moderated by warm winds off Narragansett Bay, but extremes do occur. The highest temperature ever recorded in the state was 104° Fahrenheit (40° Celsius); the lowest was −23°F (−31°C).

The state has experienced more than thirty earthquakes since the 1700s, none of them very strong. Tornadoes occur infrequently, but they have touched down at several locations in recent years. The most destructive weather events in Rhode Island have been hurricanes. Hurricanes occur less often, but are very destructive when they do appear. They are often accompanied by huge waves called *tsunamis.*

CHAPTER SIX

Here and There in Rhode Island

A statue of Roger Williams looking out at the city of Providence

The Native Americans were good trailblazers. They scouted the territory on foot and cut paths through forests, avoiding swamplands, deep streams, and steep hills. When the early colonists arrived in Rhode Island, they followed these trails with their horses and carts. Later, roads were built along many of the same trails.

Today, one can drive through all of Rhode Island on an interstate highway. The entire trip from Westerly, in the southwestern corner, up past Providence and into Massachusetts, can take less than an hour. But let's go slowly, enjoy the scenery, and explore some of the cities and towns along the way.

Greater Providence

Providence, the first settlement in Rhode Island, is the state's capital, as well as its largest city and cultural and economic center. In colonial days, Providence was second to Newport in every way, but then things changed. The Industrial Revolution brought factories

Opposite: Providence skyline

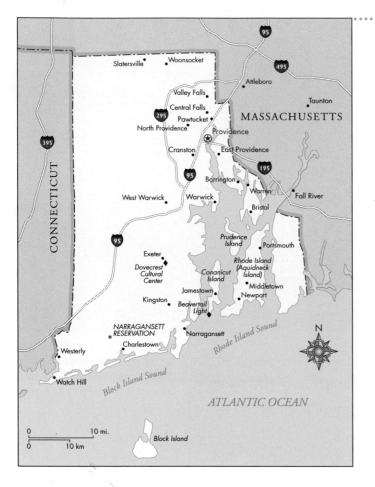

Rhode Island's cities and interstates

and people into the Blackstone Valley, north of Providence, and the city became the trading and shipping center for the state's manufactured goods.

A gold-leafed statue called *Independent Man* overlooks the city of Providence. It stands atop the dome of the Rhode Island state house, an elegant white marble building on a hill. The state house was based on the design of the U.S. Capitol. The statue symbolizes the spirit of freedom of thought and religion that has been such an important part of Rhode Island's history. Nearby, in Roger Williams National Memorial Park, is the site of a spring where Williams first decided to settle his new home.

Providence is a beautiful hilly city, filled with historic buildings, parks, and landscaped walkways. It lies along three rivers. The Moshassuck and Woonasquatucket Rivers meet near the state house, forming the Providence River that flows into Narragansett Bay.

A few years ago, much of the city was neglected and run-down. Many of its houses and public buildings were in danger of destruction. A huge city-improvement project was started in the 1980s. A great number of old buildings that reflect the city's 400-year heritage were restored.

At one time, much of the waterway was paved over. Opened and cleaned up, it is now the center of summer activities in the city. Waterplace Park, between the state house and downtown, surrounds a tidal basin in the river. There are landscaped paths and

Waterplace Park is the site of many concerts and other outdoor events.

footbridges. Concerts and special events are staged in an amphitheater. People can watch the entertainment from the river as they float along in gondolas. On special occasions during the year, fire lights up the river. A series of metal cauldrons filled with firewood mark the middle of the stream. Strains of classical music fill the air as the bonfires are set ablaze. The senses are stimulated by the sights, sounds, and smells of this alluring display. Waterfire, as the spectacle is called, blends flowing water, burning wood, and beautiful music.

Providence has the third-oldest zoo in the United States and one of the oldest libraries—the Athenaeum. The Arcade, built in 1828, was the first indoor mall in the United States.

The spectacle of Waterfire

Providence, the Name

The name *Providence* was chosen by Roger Williams shortly after he came to the region. He had endured harsh criticism from the Puritans of Massachusetts. After a difficult journey, he was greatly relieved to find a pleasant place to settle. Good, sweet freshwater was flowing from a spring. Grateful to God that his troubles appeared to be over, he decided to name his settlement Providence, "for God's merciful providence unto me in my distress." ■

More than half of Rhode Island's people live in the Providence metropolitan area. Bedroom communities surrounding the city include North Providence, East Providence, Cranston, and Warwick. Elegant estates are set among beaches and bluffs with views of Narragansett Bay.

Other Place-Names in Rhode Island

Many towns and cities in the United States are named after an explorer or founder who was important in the early history of the region. In New England, however, most place-names reflected the English colonial period, were adopted from Native American place-names, or were descriptive of the geographic location.

Kingstown, of course, honored English royalty. When Samuel Gorton founded Warwick, he named the town for an English lord who had befriended him.

Pawtucket, Narragansett, and Woonsocket are names borrowed from local Native Americans. The names Central Falls, Middletown, Newport, Portsmouth, and Westerly all describe their geographic location.

Slatersville is one Rhode Island town that is named for a family. Originally, all of northern Rhode Island was part of Providence. Gradually, separate communities became independent of Providence and chose new names. Slatersville was founded by Samuel Slater, who built the nation's first cotton mill, and his brother John. John Slater chose this small community in 1803 as a location for a gristmill, a sawmill, and a forge. Later, the Slaters also built a cotton mill here. Around it, they created the first planned mill village in the United States. Several of the early stone buildings are still standing in this pleasant little community. ■

Blackstone Valley

The Reverend William Blackstone did not bring other people to join him when he decided to settle beside the river that is named for him. He loved the rock-filled stream and its rapids and falls. No doubt he explored the deep gorge where the river flowed between great boulders. It was an idyllic spot, and apparently he was quite happy with its quiet solitude.

But when Samuel Slater looked at the Pawtucket Falls in the river, he was not thinking of the beauty of the cascade nor of the many fish he could catch in this river. He looked at the falls and

Reverend Blackstone was drawn to the rugged river that is named for him.

made plans to harness the water power to run his cotton mill. He built his first mill in 1790, in Pawtucket. In just twenty years, there were eighty-seven mills in New England, and twice that many in another five years. Pawtucket is recognized as the birthplace of the American Industrial Revolution.

All these factories needed workers. Mill villages appeared and were rapidly filled with new residents. For many years, factories hummed and clanked in the cities of Pawtucket, Central Falls, Woonsocket, and towns in between. At one time the population density— the number of people who lived in one square mile—in Central Falls was the highest in the United States.

Outdoor recreation is the greatest attraction of the Blackstone River today. People hike, ride horseback, canoe, fish, and enjoy bird-watching in several state parks.

Bristol County

A narrow peninsula points south between two bays—Narragansett and Mount Hope. This is Bristol County. Its three main towns are Barrington, Warren, and Bristol. Settlers from Plymouth Colony built a trading post near the village where Massasoit, a Wampanoag chief, lived.

The chief was friendly to the newcomers, but war

Hannah Slater

Hannah Wilkinson deserves her own place in Rhode Island's industrial history. She married Slater in 1791 and took an active part in the business. A year later, she became the first woman ever to receive a patent from the U.S. government. Her innovation was an improved process for making cotton sewing thread. ■

Along Hope Street in Bristol

between the settlers and the Wampanoag broke out after his death. His son, Metacomet, nicknamed King Philip, brought other tribes of Native Americans into a bloody war with the settlers. Most of the fighting took place in this area. It ended with the death of King Philip, in what is now Bristol. Sites of early Wampanoag villages are preserved on the woodlands of Brown University's Haffenreffer Museum of Anthropology.

Bristol's deepwater harbor helped it become a thriving commercial port before the American Revolution. By 1800, it was the fourth-busiest port in the United States. Fortunes were made from maritime trading. Merchants and shipbuilders erected grand homes and mansions, some of which are still standing. In nearby Warren, people became wealthy from the whaling industry.

Blithewold Mansion and Gardens hosts events of all kinds.

Many yachts were built at Herreshoff Boatyard, including several winners of the America's Cup. Herreshoff Marine Museum has

a collection of more than forty yachts built by the family over nearly a century.

As shipping profits declined, railroads brought a new source of income to Bristol. It became a connecting port for passengers from Boston and Providence bound for New York. Later on, the nearby village of Barrington developed as a fashionable summer spot for wealthy families.

Bristol celebrates holidays in grand style. One of the nation's largest Fourth of July parades proceeds past dozens of flag-draped homes. Summer concerts, garden displays, and other gala events are held at Blithewold Mansion and Gardens, a forty-five-room manor house built by one of Bristol's early summer residents. People come from miles around to see the city's Christmas Grand Illumination on the first Sunday in December. Visitors to Bristol County can take sightseeing cruises on Narragansett Bay from Warren.

Portsmouth, Middletown, and Jamestown

Aquidneck Island was purchased by dissenters who were expelled from the Massachusetts Bay Colony in 1638. John Clarke and William Coddington arrived first. A little later, William and Anne Hutchinson settled in the northern part of the island, which is officially named Rhode Island.

At first a farming and fishing community, Portsmouth was once the most populated town in the state. Coal was mined here for a short period of time. Today it is largely a bedroom community for commuters who work in larger towns.

One of the "creatures" on display at Green Animals

The major attraction in Portsmouth is a topiary garden called Green Animals, where eighty shrubs and trees have sculptured shapes and designs. This form of ornamental gardening is called topiary. A flowering garden forms a lovely background for twenty-one birds and animals created of yew, privet, and boxwood shrubs. A camel, elephant, giraffe, ostrich, swan, unicorn, and reindeer are among the creatures on display.

The town of Jamestown includes all of Conanicut, one of the three main islands in Narragansett Bay. The island is connected by bridges to Newport and the mainland of the state. Archaeological evidence in Jamestown indicates that people were living on the island as much as 3,000 years ago.

Jamestown was the site of one of the first lighthouses in the United States, built in 1749. A display of pictures in a cottage on the grounds illustrates the history of lighthouses. But Jamestown

The Jamestown wind-
mill was built in 1787.

has other attractions in addition to the lighthouses. A fascinating
windmill built in 1787 is still standing. Its dome can be rotated so
that the arms face the wind. The windmill powered a grain mill for
more than a hundred years.

Anne Hutchinson

Anne Hutchinson was an outspoken woman who was not afraid to challenge church authorities. She and her husband, William, were among the people who came to the Massachusetts Bay Colony in the hope of "purifying" the Anglican Church.

The Hutchinsons settled in Boston, where Anne became greatly admired for her intelligence. She raised a large family—fourteen children over a twenty-two-year period. In addition, she was active in the community, using her skills in nursing and midwifery to help other women.

Anne Hutchinson has sometimes been given credit for organizing America's first women's club. She and her husband faithfully attended church services, but she often disagreed with the sermons. She began inviting other women to meet in her home to discuss theology. Then she went even further and urged people to walk out of churches during sermons they did not agree with.

Anne was put on trial by the Anglican Church and banished from Massachusetts, along with a dozen of her followers. The Hutchinsons settled in Portsmouth, and a few years later, William Hutchinson died. Anne and her family moved to Long Island, where she was later killed by unfriendly Indians. Anne Hutchinson is remembered today as a true heroine of Rhode Island—an independent woman. ■

Newport

The city of Newport has a glorious history, with two major early chapters. In colonial days, it was the commercial, political, and cultural center of the colony. Merchants, shipowners, and shipbuilders made fortunes and built a prosperous and sophisticated city. The American Revolution brought an end to that chapter, when British troops occupied the city and nearly destroyed it.

After the war, the Industrial Revolution in the northern part of the state brought new prosperity and leadership to the city of Prov-

idence, but Newport went into a decline. Then suddenly it found new life as a resort. The nation's new millionaires discovered the city's pleasant climate and the sparkling waters surrounding it. By the end of the 1800s, Newport was America's favorite resort for the rich and famous.

The mansions along
Newport's coastline

Dozens of fabulous mansions were built along Bellevue Avenue and Ocean Drive. Some are still privately owned, but a handful of the showiest ones are open for public tours. They are Rhode Island's premier tourist attraction.

The city has also had an association with the U.S. Navy ever since the American Revolution. The Naval War College was established in Newport, as a research center, in 1884. During World War

Newport's Redwood
Library may be the
oldest library building
in the United States.

II, the city was a major center of naval activities.

The Old Stone Mill in Newport, a structure with arched walls and fine stonework, is a mystery. People have argued for years about who built it, and when. Some believe it was the work of Vikings, centuries older than any written records of Europeans in the Americas. For many years, most historians believed it was built by Rhode Island's first governor. Recently, a popular theory explains it as the creation of early Portuguese explorers in the thirteenth or fourteenth century.

Newport claims to have had the first post office in the United States, first free public school, first synagogue, first open golf tournament, and first national grass-court tennis championships. And its Redwood Library, founded in 1747, is believed to be the oldest library building in the United States.

Newport is still a resort destination, but not just for the wealthy. People come from all over to attend the summer music festivals that have added to Newport's fame. Visitors represent a wide spectrum of society. The area is popular with young adults and budget-minded vacationing families as well as with business tycoons and the elite of high society. Colorful boutiques, great seafood restaurants, yacht races, and boat tours attract tourists to its lively waterfront.

South County and Block Island

The southern part of the state is officially Washington County, but it is popularly called South County. Inland it is rural and quiet, with a few old, small villages. Sandy beaches and summer homes line the coast.

This area was the original home of the Narragansett Indians. Some descendants of the people who lived here before the European settlers arrived still live in this region. The tribe operates Dovecrest Cultural Center in Exeter. The Tomaquag Indian Memorial Museum has a collection of Northeast American Indian tribal artifacts. Special educational programs are held at the center.

An annual intertribal powwow is hosted each August by the Narragansett at tribal lands in Charlestown. The Narragansett Indian Church, built in 1859, is on the grounds, as well as the Royal Indian Burial Ground.

Watch Hill, on a point at the southwesternmost point of the state, is a community of summer houses, many of them built in the 1870s, with great views of the ocean. The Flying Horse Carousel, at the end of Bay Street, with colorful hand-carved horses, is one of the nation's oldest. A granite lighthouse built in 1856 has a small museum.

Block Island, 9 miles (14 km) offshore, was purchased from the Native Americans in 1667 by sixteen families who established a democratic settlement there. The only businesses on the island, besides tourism, have been fishing and farming. Much of the island is a nature retreat, a habitat for rare and endangered plants and animals. It can be reached by ferry, private boat, or a twenty-minute flight from Westerly.

Tourists enjoy the old hotels and the beauty of Block Island.

Opposite: The light-house at Watch Hill

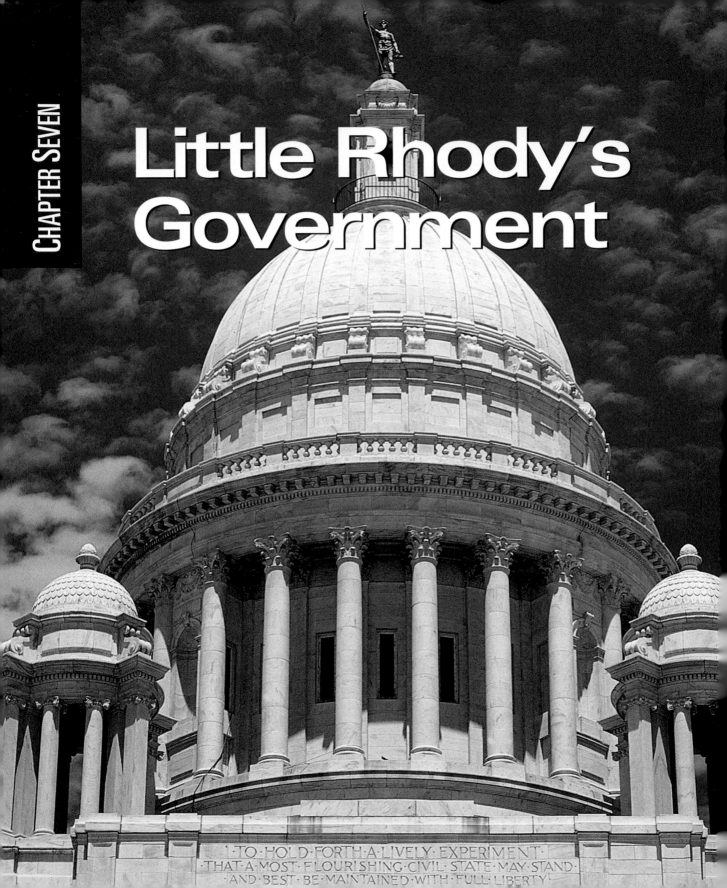

CHAPTER SEVEN

Little Rhody's Government

TO·HOLD·FORTH·A·LIVELY·EXPERIMENT·
THAT·A·MOST·FLOURISHING·CIVIL·STATE·MAY·STAND·
AND·BEST·BE·MAINTAINED·WITH·FULL·LIBERTY

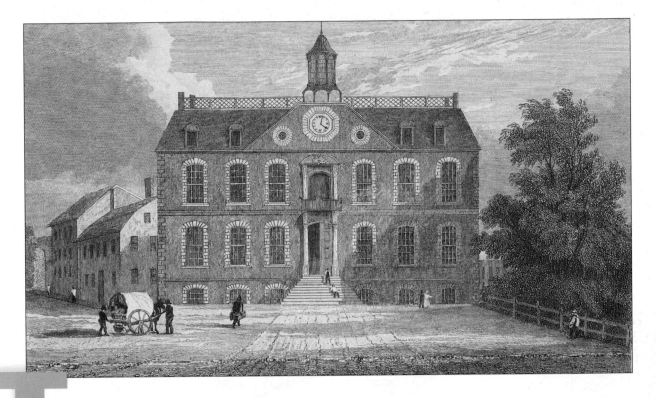

The English settlers in Rhode Island governed themselves from the very beginning. They were an English colony, but they never had a governor appointed by the king.

The original state house in Newport

In 1644, Roger Williams obtained a charter from England for "the Providence Plantations in Narragansett Bay," which set forth rules for local self-government. Decisions were made in town meetings, and local officials were elected by the people. This parliamentary charter is considered to be the colony's first constitution.

In 1663, King Charles II granted a charter for "the colony of Rhode Island and Providence Plantations." The document continued to be the basis for governing Rhode Island even after the colony declared its independence from England in 1776 and joined the Union in 1790. The original document, written on parchment, is preserved in a vault in the Rhode Island state house.

Opposite: Rhode Island's state house

Eventually Rhode Island decided to adopt a new constitution, which went into effect in 1843. This one has been amended forty-two times. A constitutional convention met in the 1980s and made a number of revisions, which were adopted in 1988.

For many years, the state government moved back and forth on a regular basis between two capitals—Newport and Providence. In 1900, Providence became the permanent capital. State officers began moving into a new capitol in December 1900, and all work on the structure was completed in 1904. The unsupported white

Rhode Island's Governors

Name	Party	Term	Name	Party	Term
Nicholas Cooke	None	1775–1778	Elisha Harris	Whig	1847–1849
William Greene	None	1778–1786	Henry B. Anthony	Whig	1849–1851
John Collins	None	1786–1790	Philip Allen	Dem.	1851–1853
Arthur Fenner	Anti-Federalist	1790–1805	Francis M. Dimond	Dem.	1853–1854
			William W. Hoppin	Whig/ Know Nothing	1854–1857
Henry Smith	Unknown	1805			
Isaac Wilbur	Unknown	1806–1807	Elisha Dyer	Rep.	1857–1859
James Fenner	Dem.-Rep.	1807–1811	Thomas G. Turner	Rep.	1859–1860
William Jones	Federalist	1811–1817	William Sprague	Dem. & Conservative	1860–1863
Nehemiah R. Knight	Dem.-Rep.	1817–1821			
William C. Gibbs	Dem.-Rep.	1821–1824	William C. Cozzens	Dem.	1863
James Fenner	Dem.-Rep.	1824–1831	James Y. Smith	Rep.	1863–1866
Lemuel H. Arnold	Nat.-Rep.	1831–1833	Ambrose E. Burnside	Rep.	1866–1869
John Brown Francis	Dem.	1833–1838	Seth Padelford	Rep.	1869–1873
William Sprague	Dem.	1838–1839	Henry Howard	Rep.	1873–1875
Samuel Ward King	R.I. Party	1840–1843	Henry Lippitt	Rep.	1875–1877
James Fenner	Law and Order	1843–1845	Charles C. Van Zandt	Rep.	1877–1880
			Alfred H. Littlefield	Rep.	1880–1883
Charles Jackson	Liberation	1845–1846	Augustus O. Bourn	Rep.	1883–1885
Byron Diman	Law and Order	1846–1847	George P. Wetmore	Rep.	1885–1887

marble dome is the second-largest in the world, after the dome of St. Peter's Basilica in Rome.

Rhode Island is represented in the federal government of the United States by two senators and two members of the House of Representatives.

At the state level, Rhode Island has three branches of government. Five state officers are elected to the executive branch: a governor, lieutenant governor, attorney general, secretary of state, and general treasurer. They serve four-year terms.

Rhode Island's Governors—*Continued*

Name	Party	Term	Name	Party	Term
John W. Davis	Dem.	1887–1888	Robert E. Quinn	Dem.	1937–1939
Royal C. Taft	Rep.	1888–1889	William H. Vanderbilt	Rep.	1939–1941
Herbert W. Ladd	Rep.	1889–1890	J. Howard McGrath	Dem.	1941–1945
John W. Davis	Dem.	1890–1891	John O. Pastore	Dem.	1945–1950
Herbert W. Ladd	Rep.	1891–1892	John S. McKiernan	Dem.	1950–1951
D. Russell Brown	Rep.	1892–1895	Dennis J. Roberts	Dem.	1951–1959
Charles W. Lippitt	Rep.	1895–1897	Christopher Del Sesto	Rep.	1959–1961
Elisha Dyer	Rep.	1897–1900	John A. Notte Jr.	Dem.	1961–1963
William Gregory	Rep.	1900–1901	John H. Chafee	Rep.	1963–1969
Charles D. Kimball	Rep.	1901–1903	Frank Licht	Dem.	1969–1973
Lucius F. C. Garvin	Dem.	1903–1905	Philip W. Noel	Dem.	1973–1977
George H. Utter	Rep.	1905–1907	J. Joseph Garrahy	Dem.	1977–1985
James H. Higgins	Dem.	1907–1909	Edward D. DiPrete	Rep.	1985–1991
Aram J. Pothier	Rep.	1909–1915	Bruce Sundlun	Dem.	1991–1995
R. Livingston Beeckman	Rep.	1915–1921	Lincoln C. Almond	Rep.	1995–
Emery J. San Souci	Rep.	1921–1923			
William S. Flynn	Dem.	1923–1925			
Aram J. Pothier	Rep.	1925–1928			
Norman S. Case	Rep.	1928–1933	Dem.-Rep.=Democratic-Republican		
Theodore F. Green	Dem.	1933–1937	Nat.-Rep.=National Republican		

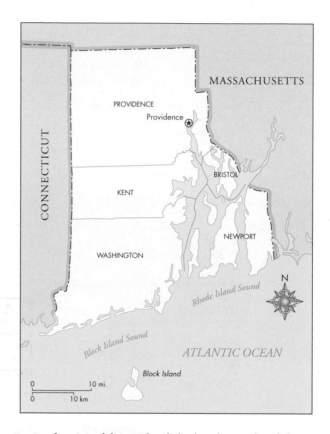

MASSACHUSETTS

PROVIDENCE

Providence ✪

CONNECTICUT

BRISTOL

KENT

NEWPORT

WASHINGTON

N

Rhode Island Sound

Block Island Sound

ATLANTIC OCEAN

Block Island

0   10 mi.
0   10 km

Rhode Island's counties

The general assembly, or legislative branch of the government, consists of two houses, a 50-member senate and a 100-member house of representatives. Legislators serve two-year terms.

Rhode Island's judicial branch consists of a supreme court, superior court, and district and family courts. The general assembly elects the justices of the supreme court to life terms and chooses one of them to be chief justice.

Local government in Rhode Island is handled by eight cities and thirty-one towns. Towns in New England are equivalent to townships in other states. The five counties in Rhode Island are

Rhode Island's State Government

Executive Branch

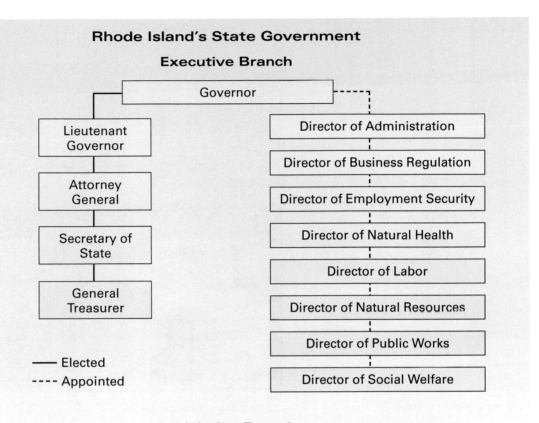

Governor

Lieutenant Governor

Attorney General

Secretary of State

General Treasurer

Director of Administration

Director of Business Regulation

Director of Employment Security

Director of Natural Health

Director of Labor

Director of Natural Resources

Director of Public Works

Director of Social Welfare

—— Elected
- - - - Appointed

Legislative Branch

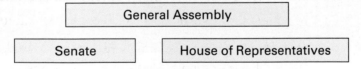

General Assembly

Senate

House of Representatives

Judicial Branch

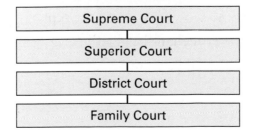

Supreme Court

Superior Court

District Court

Family Court

Rhode Island's State Symbols

State bird: Rhode Island red chicken The Rhode Island red chicken (above) is the official state bird. This breed of hen was developed in the 1850s on a farm in the town of Little Compton. Before that time, chickens were scrawny and not very tasty. The quality of the meat and eggs of the Rhode Island red made poultry-breeding an important industry. It was chosen as the official state bird in 1954. A monument commemorating the development of this chicken is on display in Little Compton.

State tree: Red maple The state tree of Rhode Island, the red maple (above), puts out clusters of red and orange flowers, hanging from reddish twigs, early each spring. The leaves are also a reddish color when they first open, gradually turning to green. It grows to a height of 60 to 80 feet (18 to 24 m) and is an excellent shade tree. The red maple is widespread in the eastern United States.

State flower: Violet Rhode Island's state flower is the violet, *viola palmata*. Violets grow wild in most parts of the world and are often planted in gardens as well. They are among the most popular of all flowers. Three other states—Illinois, New Jersey, and Wisconsin—have also named the violet their state flower.

The plants are 10 inches (25 centimeters) or less in height; the flowers have five petals. The most common varieties are deep purple or blue; other species are white and yellow. Violets appear in early spring and summer.

State mineral: Bowenite
Bowenite is a mineral found in northern Rhode Island. Named for George Bowen, the geologist who discovered it, bowenite is a semi-precious gemstone, similar to jade.

State shell: Quahog Native Americans called the thick-shelled edible clam found in Narragansett Bay a quahog (right). They used its attractive circular shell for money, or wampum. These clams are delicious, a necessary part of an authentic Rhode Island shore dinner. The quahog shell has been officially adopted as a state symbol.

State rock: Cumberlandite
Cumberlandite, a dark brown or black rock with white markings, is found on both sides of the southern part of Narragansett Bay. This rock has an interesting quality—it attracts magnets as a piece of iron does. Geologists say it is about 1 1/2 billion years old.

Rhode Island's State Flag and Seal

In 1897, Rhode Island became the third state to adopt an official state flag. The flag has a white background, with a golden anchor in the center. Underneath, a blue ribbon is inscribed with the word HOPE in gold letters. Thirteen gold stars form a circle around the anchor and the ribbon.

The seal (right) of the state of Rhode Island carries a golden anchor with the word HOPE above it. A circular border around the anchor reads:

SEAL OF THE STATE OF RHODE ISLAND AND PROVIDENCE PLANTATIONS 1636.

Rhode Island's State March
"Rhode Island"
Written by T. Clarke Brown

Here's to you, beloved Rhode
  Island
With your hills and ocean
  shore

We are proud to hail you
  "Rhody"
And your patriots of yore.
First to claim your indepen-
  dence,

Great your heritage and fame,
The smallest state in all the
  Union,
We glorify your name.

Rhode Island's State Song
"Rhode Island It's for Me"
The state song was adopted in 1996.
Words by Charlie Hall
Music by Maria Day

I've been to every state we
  have
but I think that I'm inclined,
To say that Rhody stole my
  heart;
You can keep the forty-nine.

Herring gulls that dot the sky
Blue waves that paint the rocks
Water rich with Neptune's life
The boats that line the docks.

I see the lighthouse flickering
to help the sailors see.
There is a place for everyone
Rhode Island it's for me!

Chorus:
Rhode Island, oh Rhode Island,
Surrounded by the sea
Some people roam
the earth for home
Rhode Island it's for me.

I love the October days,
The buzz on College Hill.
Harvard losing one to Brown,
A RISD student's skill.

Icicles refract the sun,
Snow falling gracefully.
Some people search
for a place that's warm

Rhode Island it's for me.
(Chorus)

The skyline piercing Providence,
The state house dome so rare.
Residents who speak their
  minds
No longer unaware.

Some people think that heaven
Is the place for ecstasy.
But don't sell short this precious
  port,
Rhode Island it's for me.
(Chorus)
(Chorus)

judicial districts only, with no local governmental authority.

Like other New England towns, most towns in Rhode Island hold annual town meetings. All voters can attend these meetings, where they elect local officials, approve local budgets, pass laws, and decide on many items of town business. This form of government, which has existed since colonial days, is one of the purest examples of democracy in the world. U.S. citizens who have lived in Rhode Island for thirty days are eligible to vote.

Lincoln Almond is Rhode Island's governor

CHAPTER EIGHT

Earning a Living

Slater Mill in
Pawtucket

Rhode Island was off to an early start in the changes brought
about by the Industrial Revolution. Factories and factory
towns rapidly replaced farms and forests. Descendants of the first
settlers—mostly of British ancestry—were soon joined by thousands of people from other European nations. Villages grew into
cities; and some of them became the most crowded cities in the
United States.

Manufacturing

At the height of Rhode Island's manufacturing era, more than half
the state's workers were employed in factories. Manufacturing
jobs have declined during most of the last hundred years, except for
boom times brought about by World Wars I and II. Today, only

Opposite: Hauling in
the day's catch

Slater Mill Historic Site

The American Industrial Revolution began in a simple two-story building in Pawtucket, Rhode Island. Slater Mill was constructed in 1793 and altered several times after that. Cotton yarn was produced here until 1905. Sunlight came into the mill through twenty-eight windows. Partitions separated areas for spinning, carding, and storage.

A dam in the Blackstone River was constructed upriver from Pawtucket Falls in 1792. Today the dam is made of brick, sheathed in wood, and anchored to natural rock. The falls still generate electricity.

A trench above the factory building drew water from the millpond to a water wheel. These landmarks can be seen today, along with a machine shop built in 1810 and the home of one of the master craftsmen who worked at the Slater Mill. The yellow clapboard mill has been restored to its 1830 appearance and is operated as a museum of industrial history. Collections of hand-operated and powered machinery illustrate the development of technology. ■

about one out of five people in the workforce are in the manufacturing sector.

However, Rhode Island factories still turn out a number of important products. Electronic machinery, transportation equipment, scientific instruments, toys, and textiles are among them. Printing and publishing, as well as food processing, are also important industries in the state.

No other state manufactures as much fashion jewelry as Rhode Island. A local goldsmith and watch repairer named Nehemiah Dodge was the father of Rhode Island's century-old jewelry industry. In 1794, he developed a method of plating cheaper metals

Davol Square is an important jewelry center.

with gold. This made it possible to create attractive and affordable jewelry. Today, more than 800 firms in the state produce jewelry, silverware, and other objects of precious metals. Among the many well-known companies in this work are Trifari, Anson, Gorham, and Speidel.

What Rhode Island Grows, Manufactures, and Mines

Agriculture	Manufacturing	Mining
Greenhouse and nursery products	Fabricated metal products	Gravel
Fishing	Jewelry	Sand
Clams	Scientific instruments	
Lobster	Silverware	
Squid		

A Shipbuilding Family and Museum

Five generations of the Herreshoff family of Bristol were engaged in shipbuilding. Their specialty was fast, beautiful yachts, but during World War II they also built patrol torpedo boats for the government.

The most coveted award in competitive yachting is the America's Cup. For more than 125 years, from 1851 to 1980, the race was always won by Americans. Yachts built by the Herreshoff Company won the prize eight times.

The Herreshoff Manufacturing Company was in business from 1863 to 1945. The Herreshoff Marine Museum (above) now stands on the site of the plant. More than forty-five craft built by Herreshoff are on display. The oldest one, the *Sprite*, was built in 1859, based on drawings sketched by Nathaniel Herreshoff when he was only sixteen years old.

A Discovery Center in the museum, run by a member of the Herreshoff family, introduces children to the world of sailing ships. Across the street from the museum is the America's Cup Hall of Fame, with photos, models, and memorabilia related to the world-famous contest. ■

Shipbuilding has been important in Rhode Island since the 1840s. Half-a-dozen companies produce yachts, boats, and ships. The Electric Boat Divison of General Dynamics Corporation makes nuclear-powered submarines for the U.S. Navy.

Agriculture, Fishing, and Mining

Only about 1 percent of Rhode Island's labor force works in agriculture and agricultural services, and 10 percent of the land in the state is used for farming. Nursery plants are the leading agricultural product. Truck gardens produce a variety of vegetables; apples, peaches, pears, and berries are grown in orchards. Vineyards, where wine grapes are grown, are a recent addition to the agricultural mix. Dairy cows, hogs, and hens are the major commercial livestock.

Cattle grazing in a Jamestown field

Lobsters and quahogs (clams) lead the list of seafood caught by commercial fishers in Rhode Island waters. In addition to several varieties of fish caught for food, many are used as bait, animal food, and fertilizer. Sand and gravel are the only mining products of any importance in the state.

Quahog Cakes

Clam cakes—a unique Rhode Island dish or appetizer—are sometimes made with quahogs, a type of ocean clam found off the coast of New England. The term *quahog* comes from an Algonquin word meaning "hard shell."

Ingredients:

      1 cup all-purpose flour
1 1/2 teaspoons baking powder
      1 teaspoon salt
      1 cup milk
      1 egg, beaten
      1 pint minced quahogs
         oil

Directions:

Mix flour, baking powder, and salt together in a large bowl. Add the milk, egg, and quahogs and stir well.

With the help of an adult, heat 3/4 inch of oil in a skillet until sizzling. Using a teaspoon, drop scoops of the quahog mixture into the oil and fry until golden brown.

Serves 4.

The U.S. Navy

The U.S. Navy was born in Rhode Island. In June 1775, two merchant ships that the Rhode Island general assembly had equipped for defense engaged in a brief battle with a British ship in Newport Harbor. Later that year, Rhode Islander Stephen Hopkins persuaded the Continental Congress to outfit thirteen armed vessels. They were called the Continental Navy, and Esek Hopkins, Stephen's brother, was commissioned as commander in chief.

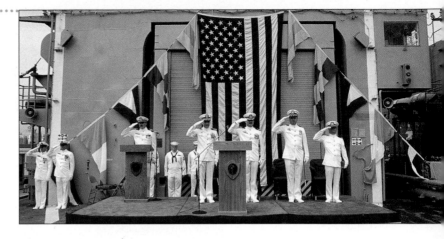

The U.S. Navy has long had a presence in Newport.

The navy is the largest employer in Newport County and the second largest in the state, after the state government. About 8,000 civilian and military personnel work for the navy. The largest commands are the Naval Education and Training Center (NETC), the Naval Underwater Systems Center, and the Naval War College. Others include the Surface Warfare Officers School, Naval Justice School, Naval Hospital Newport, Naval Dental Clinic, and Naval Legal Service Office. Several U.S. Navy ships are based in Newport.

The U.S. Naval Construction Battalion, home of the famous "Seabees," is in North Kingstown. During World War II, ninety construction battalions received their training there. These men and women provide all kinds of mobile facilities for the navy.

Transportation Services

Theodore Francis Green Airport in Warwick serves the major air-transportation needs of southeastern New England. There are five

A ferry on its way to Block Island

smaller airports in the state. Several passenger trains each day operate between New York City and Boston, with stops in Westerly, Kingston, and Providence.

Interstate 95 crosses Rhode Island diagonally from southwest to northeast. Good highways serve the entire state. Ferryboats carry passengers and goods to and from Block Island.

Who Makes Your Toys and Games?

Hasbro, Inc., is an international leader in the manufacture of toys, board games, card games, and computer games for children and adults. It was founded in Pawtucket in 1923 by two brothers—Henry and Helal Hassenfeld. The company manufactured pencil boxes and other school supplies before it moved into children's toys in the 1940s. Two of Hasbro's early popular products were Mr. Potato Head® and G.I. Joe®.

Over the years, the company has acquired other companies and product lines, including Milton Bradley and Parker Brothers. From its beginning, when the firm employed only eight people—all family members—Hasbro, Inc., has grown to a children's and family leisure-time and entertainment company with about 13,000 employees. Many of the toys and games you play with probably came from this company. ■

Port Facilities

The Port of Providence, at the head of Narragansett Bay, is one of the best deepwater harbors on the East Coast of the United States. Along with many other important cargoes, much of the fuel oil, gasoline, and kerosene used in southern New England is unloaded in Providence. The goods travel by land from there to manufacturers and consumers. Quonset Point and Newport are also important ports.

Where the Jobs Are

About one-fifth of the people working in the state of Rhode Island are in the manufacturing industry, another one-fourth in health and other services, and one-fifth in trade. The remaining workers have jobs in government, finance and insurance, construction, agriculture and mining, or are self-employed. As manufacturing jobs are lost, the service sector becomes more important.

In recent years, tourism has helped the economy by bringing visitors into the state. Some 14 million travelers visited Rhode Island in 1998. About 6 percent of the total jobs in the state are in tourism-related businesses.

MASSACHUSETTS

CONNECTICUT

Providence

Scituate Reservoir

Narragansett Bay

Worden Pond

Watchaug Pond

Rhode Island Sound

Block Island Sound

ATLANTIC OCEAN

Block Island

0 10 mi.
0 10 km

Farming
Forests, some farming
Urban area

Cattle
Clams
Corn
Dairy
Fish
Fruit
Hay
Lobster
Manufacturing
Nursery products
Potatoes
Poultry
Vegetables

CHAPTER NINE

The People of Rhode Island

Diversity is Rhode Island's heritage. From the earliest colonists to the latest immigrants from eastern Europe and southeast Asia, Rhode Island has been a place for people who seek the freedom to be themselves.

The first colonists were, for the most part, English Puritans from Massachusetts and Connecticut. Within a few years,

People of all backgrounds have made their home in Rhode Island.

they were joined by small groups of Quakers, Jews, French Huguenots, and other Europeans. All these groups found ways to make a living by farming, fishing, shipbuilding, and trade.

When factories began to spring up along the rivers in northern Rhode Island, life in the young state changed drastically. The word spread that factories needed more workers. People from other countries began to flock to Rhode Island. It was a land of opportunity, where jobs were plentiful.

Only a few of today's Rhode Islanders are descended from original Yankee stock, but all the residents share a pride in the state's early history and its tradition of tolerance and respect for differences. The state's culture has been enriched by the customs, lifestyles, ethics, religions, skills, and foods that originated in many different countries.

Opposite: Watching a parade in Bristol

Rhode Islanders celebrate their heritage and their history.

Population of Rhode Island's Major Cities (1990)

Providence	160,728
Warwick	85,427
Cranston	76,060
Pawtucket	72,644
East Providence	50,380
Woonsocket	43,877

Ethnic Backgrounds

The need for factory workers prompted several waves of immigration to Rhode Island. In the 1820s, most of the newcomers were from Ireland. Years later, during the Civil War, many people of French descent moved south from Canada to join the tide of new factory workers. Others, fewer in numbers, came from Sweden, Germany, Portugal, and the Cape Verde islands.

Another wave of immigration began in the 1890s. This one brought many Italians, as well as Poles, Russians, Greeks, Armenians, Syrians, Lebanese, Ukrainians, and Lithuanians. A few years later, in the 1920s, Congress passed laws that severely limited immigration for a while. From 1950 on, African-Americans from the south, Hispanics from Caribbean countries, and refugees from Southeast Asia added more ethnic diversity to Rhode Island.

About two-thirds of the residents of Rhode Island today are Roman Catholics. This is the highest percentage of any state.

The 1990 U.S. Census counted less than 10 percent of the population of Rhode Island as foreign-born. But 60 percent reported their ancestry to be either Irish, Italian, or French Canadian, the three largest ethnic groups. Fewer than 20 percent said they were of English descent.

Rhode Island's population density

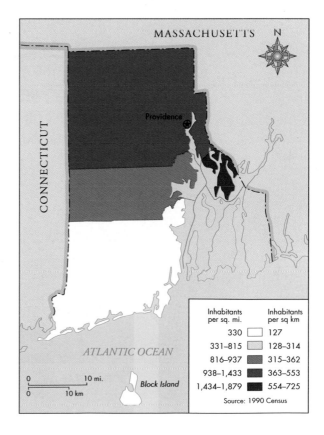

Where They Live

Rhode Island's population is not evenly divided. Nearly nine out of every ten people in the state live in cities, with more than half of them in the northeastern part of the state. The cities of Central Falls, Cranston, East Providence, Newport, Pawtucket, Providence, Warwick, and Woonsocket have some of the most densely populated sections in the United States.

The rest of the people are scattered in small, rural villages and farmlands. About 60 percent of Rhode Island is forestland. Differences between urban and rural lifestyles and economic needs are great, but the small size of the state helps to bridge these differences.

Schools and Libraries

The people who settled the New England colonies had a high regard for education. They established schools as soon as they possibly could. Ministers often started schools for boys. Women teachers operated "dame schools," where they taught girls and very young boys.

In 1640, a man named Robert Lenthal came to Newport "to keep a public school for learning of the youth." This school is considered to be one of the first public schools in the colonies.

State laws to establish and pay for public schools were passed in the 1800s. In 1845 the first parochial schools in Rhode Island were started. At one time, one out of every four Rhode Island students attended a Catholic school.

A state board of education was founded in 1870. By then, the state had six public high schools and many private academies. Shortly after that, a school tax law was established, "for the benefit of all the children of all the people." Today, children between the ages of five and fifteen in Rhode Island are required to attend school.

In addition to school libraries, there are forty-five public libraries in the state, as well as numerous private, college, and university libraries.

Colleges and Universities

Brown University, in Providence, is the seventh-oldest college in the United States. Founded by a group of Baptists, it was chartered as Rhode Island College in 1764, in Warren. The school moved to

Providence in 1770 and was later renamed Brown University. A major research center, it is ranked among the nation's twenty-five best graduate schools. Brown's library collections include more than a million volumes.

In 1775, a beautiful new Baptist Church was built in Providence, and Brown University's commencement exercises have been held there ever since, even though the school has no direct ties to the Baptist Church today.

Rhode Island School of Design, also in Providence, is one of the leading design colleges in the United States. Courses include fine and industrial arts, design, and architecture. Many art students come from all over the world to study at this school. Extension classes are held for students of all ages, including Saturday classes for grade school and high school children. College students may take part in a European honors program, which includes study in Rome, Italy.

Brown University is a well-respected school in Providence.

The University of Rhode Island, in Kingston, has outstanding programs in oceanography, ocean engineering, marine-related research, and environmental education and research. Johnson and Wales University, in Providence, is nationally known for its culinary arts program. Some of the nation's best chefs are trained here.

Art students from around the world study at the Rhode Island School of Design.

Computer sciences and technology, are emphasized at New England Institute of Technology; business courses are taught at Bryant College; and arts and sciences are offered at several other private and state-supported colleges. The Naval War College, established in 1884, is the oldest institution of its kind in the world.

Rhode Island Food

People from dozens of countries, in all corners of the world, have brought their native traditions, recipes, and favorite spices to Rhode Island. Just about any kind of cuisine can be enjoyed in the state's many restaurants. Perhaps the two most popular are Italian and Portuguese, but Caribbean, Mediterranean, and Asian cooking are not hard to find.

A few dishes, though, are proudly described as being purely Rhode Island. One is quahog (pronounced KO-hog locally) chowder. If a tourist calls it clam chowder, a Rhode Islander is apt to correct the speaker. True, a quahog is a clam, but it is not just any old clam.

It is a particular clam native to Narragansett Bay. And Rhode Island quahog chowder is not the same as New England chowder, which is made with milk, or Manhattan chowder, which includes tomatoes. Rhode Island quahog chowder is made in a clear broth.

But quahog chowder is only one of many ways to fix this delicious morsel of seafood. Quahogs can be steamed, fried, or baked. There are quahog cakes, quahog pie, and stuffed quahogs, or "stuffies." Visitors can sample all of these at the International Quahog Festival in Wickford, held each August. There's even a stuffie cooking contest.

Traditional Rhode Island shore dinners can be held at the beach—or anywhere else.

A selection at the International Quahog Festival

The menu will include quahogs fixed in several different ways, as well as baked sausage, lobster, corn on the cob, watermelon, and Indian pudding—a steamed pudding made of cornmeal and molasses.

In some places, "johnny cake" just means cornbread. In Rhode Island, a johnny cake is cooked on a griddle like a pancake, but it is made of cornmeal.

What does a Rhode Islander drink to wash down all this wonderful food? The favorite drink is coffee milk, sometimes called a cabinet. It's just like chocolate milk, except that it is flavored with coffee syrup instead of chocolate. In Rhode Island, coffee milk is not merely popular—it's the official state drink.

CHAPTER TEN

Enjoying Leisure Time

Rhode Island's beaches provide the scene for hours of fun.

Hiking, biking, boating, swimming, beachcombing, and just enjoying nature are a few of the most popular ways to spend free time in the little state of Rhode Island. Every part of the state is close to Narragansett Bay, the ocean, and the countryside.

Entertainment comes in many forms: plays, musicals, concerts, opera, even a one-of-a-kind circus, the Pan-Twilight Circus in Newport. Yacht races, fishing tournaments, and spectator sports are other popular of leisure-time activities.

Theater

Theater seems to be almost everywhere. Performers range from big-name stars to students and members of amateur community theaters. Some of Rhode Island's theaters have been in business for much of the twentieth century.

Opposite: Fishing in Newport

One of the oldest groups is the Community Players of Pawtucket. Organized in 1920, the group presents four productions a year, usually musicals or comedies.

Summer theater is a widespread tradition in New England. Matunuck's Theater-by-the-Sea has been bringing professional performers to Rhode Island's South Coast since 1933. Performances are staged in an old barn, a restored building that is on the National Register of Historic Places. Besides the principal schedule, a children's festival in late summer features daytime shows.

The much younger Colonial Theater in Westerly, housed in a nineteenth-century Greek Revival church, also presents a varied summer program, including specials for children. The season features drama, comedy, and musicals, plus seasonal presentations between Thanksgiving and Christmas and performances of Shakespeare in the Park in July.

The Blackstone River Theatre in Central Falls offers a variety of entertainment throughout the year. Local theater groups perform here, including a folk ensemble known as Pendragon. This group showcases the diversity of immigrant groups that have settled in the Blackstone Valley. Concerts of jazz, blues, and ethnic music are staged here, as well as many programs for children.

Several active theaters and theater groups make Providence a busy center of entertainment. Operas, concerts, and Broadway shows are frequently staged at the Ocean State Performing Arts Center in Providence. The building, a beautiful 1928 movie palace restored to its original glittering splendor, is a wonderful setting for fine entertainment.

The Trinity Repertory Company, also in downtown Providence, is New England's oldest resident theater company. Both classic and modern works are performed here. Harrisville, a tiny settlement in northwestern Rhode Island, also has a resident theater company that performs in a brick building behind the library. Other theater companies include the Rhode Island Shakespeare Theatre in Newport, the Puppet Workshop in Providence, and the Warwick Musical Theatre.

An outdoor concert in Providence

Music

Several summer music festivals in Newport are famous worldwide. The two-week Newport Music Festival presents more than fifty concerts of chamber music in several of the city's historic mansions. Jazz Festival Newport and the Newport Folk Festival attract some of the best-known artists and thousands of listeners.

The University of Rhode Island hosts a summer chamber-music festival in Kingston. Outdoor concerts are presented in East Providence, Bristol, and North Kingstown. A summer pops concert in Westerly is an all-day affair. A local chorus and high school band perform, followed by the Boston Festival Orchestra playing the 1812 Overture with a rousing finale of fireworks and church bells. The Rhode Island Historical Society presents "Concerts on the Lawn" from July to September. The Rhode Island Philharmonic

The Face on the Dollar Bill

One of America's most famous early portrait painters was born in North Kingstown, Rhode Island, in 1755. You may not know his name, but you have seen copies of one of Gilbert Stuart's paintings many, many times—the portrait of President George Washington that appears on the one-dollar bill.

Stuart (left) studied art in London, and returned to the United States in 1793. He soon became known as the finest portrait painter in the nation. He painted portraits of the first five presidents. His three likenesses of Washington were so much in demand that he created more than 100 copies of them. The original of the portrait used on the dollar bill hangs in the Museum of Fine Arts in Boston, Massachusetts. The Gilbert Stuart Birthplace, on Gilbert Stuart Road north of Saunderstown, is open to the public. ■

Orchestra, the Philharmonic Youth Orchestra, and the Young People's Symphony of Rhode Island perform programs of classical music to enthusiastic listeners.

Museums

Rhode Island School of Design has an outstanding art museum. More than 75,000 works are in its permanent collection, including examples of art styles throughout history. American antiques are on display there, including Newport silver and cabinet work, as well as French impressionist paintings, Greek bronzes, and Roman tiles and mosaics.

There are more than thirty-five galleries in the state. Gallery Night is celebrated once a month in Providence, when a free trolley shuttles visitors to a dozen or so galleries, antique shops, and museums.

A most unusual museum—probably the only one of its kind in the world—is the Johnson and Wales Culinary Archives and

H. P. Lovecraft

Anyone who likes horror tales and movies knows about the work of Providence author H. P. Lovecraft. He has been called the greatest writer of weird and supernatural stories since Edgar Allan Poe. He wrote about all kinds of monsters who lived in macabre societies of his own invention. Many of the tales were set in New England.

Lovecraft had a rather lonely childhood. He read a lot of gothic tales, and then began to make up his own. Quite a few were published in *Weird Tales* magazine. The writer died at the early age of forty-seven. ■

A display at the Johnson and Wales Culinary Archives and Museum

Museum, in Providence. Johnson and Wales University is famous for its courses in food and hospitality; its museum has more than half a million items related to these subjects. On exhibit are documents, such as a dinner invitation issued by President Thomas Jefferson, menus from everywhere, and old postcards featuring restaurants. In addition, there are primitive Native American cooking stones, spoons and other objects from ancient Egypt and Rome, antique cookstoves, and many more food-related objects.

The Providence Children's Museum is a treasure-house of exhibits and activities. One of the most popular is a simulated travel through time. Special films and story-telling programs for youngsters are given regularly at the Providence Athenaeum, one of the oldest libraries in the United States.

African-Americans have lived in Rhode Island since the early days of the slave trade. The history of black Rhode Islanders is told through exhibits at the Rhode Island Black Heritage Society Museum in Providence. One of its exhibits features the First Black Regiment of Rhode Island, which took part in the American Revolution.

A collection of dolls made over the past 300 years is on display at Newport's Doll Museum. For those who prefer to get close to live creatures, the Newport Aquarium specializes in the aquatic animals of Narragansett Bay. Young visitors are encouraged to touch the eels, crabs, and fish and also to carry some of them back to the shore and set them free.

Other Newport museums include the Art Museum, which has a permanent collection of nineteenth- and twentieth-century American art. The Naval War College Museum has exhibits about the history of the U.S. Navy in this region.

The Redwood Library and Athenaeum, built in 1750, is the state's oldest library. Many of the books it contained when it first opened are still kept there. The Athenaeum art collection includes paintings by Gilbert Stuart and Rembrandt Peale.

The start of a race off the Newport coast

Yachting and Tennis

Newport, Rhode Island, means two things in the sports world—yachting and tennis. For more than fifty years, from 1930 to 1983, the world-famous America's Cup races were held off Newport's shores.

A brick building on the waterfront houses the Museum of Yachting. Photos, paintings, models, gear, artifacts, and other displays trace the history of yachting. The museum's ship *Shamrock V* is usually moored outside or at sea nearby. Newport hosts regattas and other boating events throughout the sailing season.

The International Tennis Hall of Fame is in a historic structure built in 1880. The Newport Casino was a social and recreational club for the wealthy people who vacationed in Newport at that time. There are thirteen grass courts, said to be the oldest such courts in continuous use in the world.

The International Tennis Hall of Fame in Newport.

Baseball

Pawtucket is the home of Rhode Island's only professional sports team. The Pawsox (Pawtucket Red Sox) are a minor-league farm team of the Boston Red Sox. The team's many loyal fans crowd into McCoy Stadium, and youngsters compete with one another to collect autographs from team members.

College and High School Sports

Two Rhode Island basketball teams, the Providence College Friars and the University of Rhode Island Rams square off each season in a hotly contested match. Both teams have had very good records in recent years. Football teams from these colleges and from Brown University also draw crowds each fall.

Hockey is popular in Rhode Island, especially in Woonsocket. Three players on that city's Mount Saint Charles Academy team—Mathieu Schneider, Brian Berard, and Keith Carney—were members of the U. S. Olympic hockey team in Nagano, Japan, in 1998.

Gravity Games

A new type of competitive sports event premiered in Providence in the summer of 1999. Televised on NBC, the Gravity Games

Mathieu Schneider is one of three Rhode Island hockey players to make the 1998 U.S. Olympic team.

A Two-Month-Long Baseball Game

McCoy Stadium holds the record for the longest professional baseball game in history. The game between the Pawsox and the Rochester Red Wings began on April 18, 1981, and was suspended at 4:09 A.M., April 19. The score was tied, 2–2. Two months later, the two teams met again to finish the game. This time, in the thirty-third inning, the Pawsox were victorious. ■

included various stunt bicycling, inline skating, skateboarding, street luge, wakeboarding, and freestyle motocross sports. The city prepared innovative downhill, vertical, and street courses to stage the events.

Television and Film

A movie filmed largely in Newport and a popular television show set in Providence have given a glimpse of these Rhode Island cities to the viewing public. Courthouse scenes in Steven Spiel-

Cast of the NBC program *Providence* (left to right): Concetta Tomei, Paula Cale, Mike Farrell, Melina Kanakaredes, and Seth Peterson

The state hosts all kinds of festivals throughout the year.

berg's 1997 epic movie *Amistad* were shot in Newport's historic (1739) Colony House. *Providence* is about a doctor who returns home to live with her father and siblings.

Festivals

Rhode Islanders love to spend their leisure time at festivals—sports events, holiday events, ethnic festivals, and historic commemorations. French Canadians hold a jubilee in Woonsocket in August; the patron saint of Italy is honored in May at the Feast of

St. Joseph, in Providence; and the American Indian Federation holds a powwow in August in West Greenwich.

Rhode Island is made up of people from many backgrounds and many walks of life, and its diversity has added to the spirit of its residents. This spirit is summed up in the Latin words that are carved around the interior of the dome in the Rhode Island state house. The words mean: "The times are happy when it is permitted to think as you like and say what you think."

A Portuguese celebration in Providence

Timeline

United States History

The first permanent English settlement is established in North America at Jamestown. **1607**

Pilgrims found Plymouth Colony, the second permanent English settlement. **1620**

America declares its independence from Britain. **1776**

The Treaty of Paris officially ends the Revolutionary War in America. **1783**

The U.S. Constitution is written. **1787**

Rhode Island State History

1524 Giovanni da Verrazzano sails into what is now Narragansett Bay.

1636 Roger Williams arrives in what is now Rhode Island and founds Providence.

1644 England gives Roger Williams a charter for Rhode Island.

1647 Providence, Warwick, Portsmouth, and Newport unite.

1663 England grants the colonists the Charter of Rhode Island and Providence Plantations.

1675 Under Metacomet, Native Americans attack settlers in Rhode Island and Massachusetts and burn down many of the towns.

1764 Rhode Island soldiers fire a cannon at British vessels in Narragansett Bay, beginning one of the first battles in the Revolutionary War.

1774 Slaves are prohibited from entering Rhode Island.

1775 The first U.S. Navy is formed after Rhode Island's general assembly outfits two ships of war.

1776 Rhode Island breaks away from its affiliation with Britain.

1790 Rhode Island becomes the thirteenth state on May 29.

United States History

The Louisiana Purchase almost **1803**
doubles the size of the United States.

The United States and Britain **1812–15**
fight the War of 1812.

The North and South fight **1861–65**
each other in the American Civil War.

The United States is **1917–18**
involved in World War I.

The stock market crashes, **1929**
plunging the United States into
the Great Depression.

The United States **1941–45**
fights in World War II.

The United States becomes a **1945**
charter member of the U.N.

The United States **1951–53**
fights in the Korean War.

The U.S. Congress enacts a series of **1964**
groundbreaking civil rights laws.

The United States **1964–73**
engages in the Vietnam War.

The United States and other **1991**
nations fight the brief
Persian Gulf War against Iraq.

Rhode Island State History

1843 The state adopts a new constitution
after the Dorr Rebellion in 1842.

1938 A hurricane hits Rhode Island, killing
more than 250 people and destroying
millions of dollars worth of property.

1969 The Newport Bridge spanning Narragansett Bay opens. Interstate 95 is
completed across the state.

1971 Personal income taxes are adopted in
the state.

Fast Facts

Rhode Island's state house

Rhode Island red chicken

Statehood date   May 29,1790, the 13th state

Official state name   State of Rhode Island and Providence Plantations

Origin of state name   Exact origin unknown. One theory is that Giovanni da Verrazzano reported finding an island about the size of Rhodes—a Greek island—in 1524. Others believe the state was named *Roode Eylandt* (Red Island) by Dutch explorer Adriaen Block because of its red clay.

State capital   Providence

State nickname   Little Rhody, The Ocean State

State motto   Hope

State bird   Rhode Island red chicken

Red maple

State flower	Violet
State rock	Cumberlandite
State mineral	Bowenite
State shell	Quahog
State song	"Rhode Island It's for Me"
State tree	Red maple
State fair	Richmond (mid-August)
Total area; rank	1,231 sq. mi. (3,188 sq km); 50th
Land; rank	1,045 sq. mi. (2,707 sq km); 50th
Water; rank	186 sq. mi. (482 sq km); 48th
Inland water; **rank**	168 sq. mi. (435 sq km); 46th
Coastal water; **rank**	18 sq. mi. (47 sq km); 20th
Geographic center	Kent, 1 mile (1.6 km) southwest of Crompton
Latitude and longitude	Rhode Island is located approximately between 49° 09′ and 42° 03′ N and 71° 08′ and 71° 53′ W
Highest point	Jerimoth Hill, 812 feet (248 m) above sea level
Lowest point	Sea level along the Atlantic coast
Largest city	Providence
Number of counties	5
Population; rank	1,005,984 (1990 census); 43rd
Density	829 persons per sq. mi. (320 per sq km)
Population distribution	86% urban, 14% rural

Rhode Island coastline

Ethnic distribution (does not equal 100%)	White	91.11%
	Hispanic	5.09%
	African-American	4.50%
	Asian and Pacific Islanders	2.00%
	Native American	0.40%
Record high temperature	104°F (40°C) at Providence on August 2, 1975	
Record low temperature	–23°F (–31°C) at Kingston on January 11, 1942	
Average July temperature	71°F (22°C)	
Average January temperature	29°F (–2°C)	
Average annual precipitation	44 inches (112 cm)	

Statue of Roger Williams

Natural Areas and Historic Sites

National Heritage Corridor

Blackstone River Valley National Heritage Corridor allows tourists to see the origins of the Industrial Revolution in the United States. Extending from Providence to Worcester, Massachusetts, this area has the ruins of factories, canals, mill villages, and many other remnants of American ingenuity that moved the United States into the twentieth century.

National Memorial

Roger Williams National Memorial honors Rhode Island's founder. The memorial stands on the first Rhode Island settlement.

Narragansett Bay

National Historic Sites

Touro Synagogue National Historic Site commemorates the first synagogue in the United States. Its congregation, originally founded in 1658, is still active.

State Beaches

There are four state beaches in Rhode Island: East Matunuk State Beach, Misquamicut State Beach, Salty Brine State Beach, and Roger W. Wheeler State Beach. Also popular with tourists are East Beach and the Charlestown Beachway.

State Parks

Rhode Island has eleven state parks. World War II Memorial State Park in Woonsocket is dedicated to the veterans of that war as well as Korean and Vietnam War veterans. Beavertail State Park in Jamestown offers beach buffs the chance to walk or drive along the beach. It also has some of the best saltwater fishing in the state. The western boundary of Colt State Park in Bristol is completely open to Narragansett Bay, offering sightseers a breathtaking view of the water. It offers the Chapel-by-the-Sea, as well as picnic areas and many fields for playing.

Sports Teams

NCAA Teams (Division 1)

Brown University Bears

Providence College Friars

University of Rhode Island Rams

Cultural Institutions

Libraries

The Providence Public Library has numerous specialized collections and programs for the public. These include reading programs, the Littman Art Collection, and the Rhode Island Collection.

Redwood Library

The Rhode Island State Archives contain materials on the state's history, including documents dating back to 1638, along with thousands of photographs.

University Library, at the University of Rhode Island in Kingston, offers its Special Collections Department, which contains the University Archives, Rhode Island Collection, Rare Book Collection, Manuscript Collection, and a collection of interviews on local history.

Museums

The Museum of Natural History in Providence has a fantastic collection of insects, birds, and fossils, along with an exhibit on geology. Cormack Planetarium, part of the museum, has a telescope for viewing the moon, day or night.

The Rhode Island Black Heritage Society has information on the history of African-Americans in Rhode Island, including photographs, paintings, documents, manuscripts, and letters.

The Rhode Island School of Design Museum holds more than 75,000 pieces of art, ranging from impressionist paintings to Chinese sculpture. It also has an Egyptian gallery with an actual coffin and mummy.

Rose Island Lighthouse in Newport offers day and night tours of the lighthouse, giving visitors a chance to see its inner workings. Nighttime visitors can stay overnight and relive lighthouse-keeping in its early days, along with helping to run the lights.

Rhode Island School of Design

Performing Arts

Rhode Island has one major symphony orchestra and one major professional theater company.

Universities and Colleges

In the mid-1990s, Rhode Island had three public and eleven private institutions of higher learning.

A Rhode Island
celebration

Annual Events

January–March

New Year's Day Plunge events in Newport, Wickford, and
Jamestown (January)

Winter Sports Carnival in Providence (February)

Irish Heritage Month in Newport (March)

April–June

May Breakfasts around the state (May)

Festival of Historic Houses in Providence (June)

Gaspee Days Colonial Encampment in Warwick (June)

Newport–Bermuda Yacht Race (biennially in June)

Providence Festival Chorus Concert (June)

July–September

Bristol Fourth of July Parade

Black Ships Festival in Newport (July)

Invitation Block Island Sound Race at Watch Hill (July)

Hall of Fame Tennis Championships in Newport (July)

Newport Music Festival (July)

Rhode Island Red Chicken Barbecue in Little Compton (July)

Wickford Art Festival (July)

Annual International Invitation Tennis Tournament in Newport
(August)

Atlantic Tuna Tournament at Block Island (August)

Ben & Jerry's Folk Festival in Newport (August)

Charlestown Chamber Seafood Festival (August)

International Quahog Festival in Wickford (August)

JVC Jazz Festival in Newport (August)

The lighthouse at
Watch Hill

Rhode Island Open Salt-Water Fishing Derby (August)

Providence Waterfront Festival (September)

October–December

Autumnfest in Woonsocket (October)

Antique Auto Tour, Woonsocket to Westerly (October)

Scituate Art Festival (October)

Heritage Day Pow Wow in Warwick (November)

First Night Providence (December)

Famous People

Nelson Wilmarth Aldrich (1841–1915)	Public official
Zachariah Allen (1795–1882)	Inventor
Nicholas Brown (1729–1791)	Manufacturer
Ruth Ann Buzzi (1936–)	Actor and comedian
William Ellery Channing (1780–1842)	Religious leader
George Michael Cohan (1878–1942)	Composer and actor
George William Curtis (1824–1892)	Author and lecturer
Thomas Wilson Dorr (1805–1854)	Lawyer and political reformer
Robert Gray (1755–1806)	Explorer
Nathanael Greene (1742–1786)	Revolutionary War soldier
Stephen Hopkins (1707–1785)	Colonial administrator
Anne Hutchinson (1591–1643)	Religious dissident
Napoleon (Larry) Lajoie (1874–1959)	Baseball player
Howard Phillips (H. P.) Lovecraft (1890–1937)	Author
Matthew Calbraith Perry (1794–1858)	Naval officer

Nicholas Brown

Oliver Hazard Perry (1785–1819)   Naval officer

Gilbert Charles Stuart (1755–1828)   Artist

Abraham Tourro (1777?–1822)   Merchant and philanthropist

Roger Williams (1603?–1683)   Clergyman and colonial leader

Roger Williams

To Find Out More

History

- Fradin, Dennis Brindell. *Rhode Island*. Chicago: Childrens Press, 1995.

- Fradin, Dennis Brindell. *The Rhode Island Colony*. Chicago: Childrens Press, 1989.

- Macauley, David. *Mill*. New York: Houghton Mifflin, 1983.

- Thompson, Kathleen. *Rhode Island*. Austin, Tex.: Raintree/Steck Vaughn, 1996.

- Warner, J. F. *Rhode Island*. Minneapolis: Lerner Publications, 1993.

Fiction

- Curtis, Alice Turner. *Little Maid of Narragansett Bay*. Bedford, Mass.: Applewood, 1998.

- Nicholson, Peggy. *The Case of the Squeaky Thief*. Minneapolis: Lerner Publications, 1994.

Biographies

- Avi, James Watling. *Finding Providence: The Story of Roger Williams*. New York: HarperCollins, 1997.

- Everett, Gwen. *John Brown: One Man against Slavery*. New York: Rizzoli, 1993.

- Nichols, Joan Kane. *A Matter of Conscience: The Trial of Anne Hutchinson*. Austin, Tex.: Raintree/Steck Vaughn, 1992.

Websites

■ **The City of Providence**
http://www.providenceri.com/
The website for Rhode Island's capital city

■ **Online Office of the Secretary of State**
http://www.state.ri.us/
For information about state government and history

■ **Visit Rhode Island**
http://visitrhodeisland.com/index2.html
The official site of the state's department of tourism

Addresses

■ **Haffenreffer Museum of Anthropology**
Brown University
300 Tower Street
Bristol, RI 02809
For information about the museum dedicated to human cultures

■ **The Rhode Island Historical Society**
110 Benevolent Street
Providence, RI 02906
For information on state history

■ **The State House Library**
State House
Providence, RI 02903
For information on the government and its history

Index

Page numbers in *italics* indicate illustrations.

Meet the Author

Sylvia McNair was born in Korea and believes she inherited a love of travel from her missionary parents. She grew up in Vermont. After graduating from Oberlin College, she held a variety of jobs, married, had four children, and settled in the Chicago area. She now lives in Evanston, Illinois.

"New England is my favorite section of the United States. I've always been interested in its history and loved its scenery. I've lived for brief periods of time in five of the six New England states. Many years ago, I spent a year in Providence writing scripts for radio programs about Rhode Island. I have a lot of happy memories.

"Writing a book about a specific state or country gives me the chance to learn as much as I can about the subject. I read, interview people, and see what I can find on the Internet. When I'm reading or writing about a particular place, I'm really there, in my imagination. Each state has its own history, landscape, and personality. I hope this book will give young people a desire to learn more about Rhode Island and other states."

Sylvia McNair has traveled in all fifty states and more than forty countries. She is the author of several travel guides and more than twenty books for young people published by Children's Press.

Photo Credits